NORMAN O'NEILL.

A Life of Music

yours always

Norman O'Neill

NORMAN O'NEILL

A Life of Music

BY

DEREK HUDSON

AUTHOR OF

"THOMAS BARNES OF 'THE TIMES'" "BRITISH JOURNALISTS AND NEWSPAPERS"
"A POET IN PARLIAMENT (LIFE OF W. M. PRAED)"

MYTYL : What are those people doing who are making
such a noise ? . . .
TYLTYL : They're the musicians.
MYTYL : Are they angry ? . . .
TYLTYL : No ; but it's hard work.

The Blue Bird.

Quality Press Ltd
Publishers
18 Adam Street
Adelphi London
W C 2

To

ADINE, PATRICK AND YVONNE

First published 1945

THIS BOOK IS PRODUCED IN
COMPLETE CONFORMITY WITH THE
AUTHORIZED ECONOMY STANDARDS

MADE AND PRINTED IN GREAT BRITAIN BY MORRISON AND GIBB LTD.,
PRINTERS, TANFIELD, EDINBURGH, AND PUBLISHED BY QUALITY PRESS LTD.,
18 ADAM STREET, ADELPHI, LONDON, W.C.2

CONTENTS

5

ILLUSTRATIONS

INTRODUCTION

THE year 1934 was a year of tragic loss for British music. On February 23, Sir Edward Elgar died. Norman O'Neill died on March 3. On May 23 died Gustav Holst; and on June 10 Frederick Delius. Biographies of three of these outstanding figures in the musical life of the nation have already appeared. As a composer, Norman O'Neill worked on a smaller scale than Elgar, Holst, or his great friend Delius, but in many ways his life lends itself more easily to biography—there was in it more incident and variety than commonly fall to the lot of composers.

Although many of his concert works were heard at the Queen's Hall from 1901 onwards, and although he wrote chamber music and a large number of songs and piano pieces, it is for his work in the theatre that Norman O'Neill is chiefly remembered. His compositions for *The Blue Bird*, for Lord Dunsany's plays, for *Mary Rose* and *A Kiss for Cinderella*, and for *Kismet*, are only a few that stand out in the stream of theatre music that came from his studio over a period of more than thirty years. He wrote music for several Shakespeare plays, and at the time of his untimely death he was about to concentrate on this branch of his art— which, as a lover of Shakespeare, particularly appealed to him. In all his work he never forsook the high standard of craftsmanship which was associated with his name.

No one has done more in this century to raise the level of our theatre music than O'Neill, and it follows that his influence on the general musical taste of the country has been considerable. This influence he also brought to bear, less obviously but no less actually, through his work as treasurer of the Royal Philharmonic Society; while as a teacher at the Royal Academy of Music he sought to pass on to a new generation those secrets of the technique of composition which he had so thoroughly mastered. His marriage with a distinguished pianist and teacher resulted in a musical partnership unique in our day. If these are not in themselves sufficient reasons for this biography, there is a further justification that must be decisive : that many will be glad to have a memorial of one of the most charming and best loved men of his time.

Many thanks are due to my mother-in-law, Mrs. Norman O'Neill; to my wife, Norman O'Neill's daughter; and to Mr.

Frank B. O'Neill, his brother, for all the help they have given me.

The list of Norman O'Neill's friends and acquaintances who have helped in one way or another is a long one, but I should like particularly to express my obligation to Mr. George Baker, Mr. Ernest Irving, Mr. Balfour Gardiner, Mr. J. Mewburn Levien, Mr. Frederic Austin, Mr. K. A. Wright, Mr. Francis Toye, Miss A. E. Keeton, Colonel Stanley Bell, Mr. Charles La Trobe, Mr. Ernest Milton, Mr. Leslie Bridgewater, Mr. Archie de Bear, Mr. Ashley Dukes, Mrs. Margaret Vessey, Miss Margaret Drew,—and the late Sir Henry Wood who, in the last months of his life, wrote to me : " I assure you I held Norman O'Neill's work in the greatest respect, and admired him as an artist and colleague."

I am also grateful for their consent to the publication of letters or extracts, to Mr. Eric Fenby and Messrs. G. Bell (publishers of *Delius as I knew him*, by Eric Fenby) ; to Messrs. Putnam (publishers of *Poems : 1918–1923*, by E. Temple Thurston) ; to Mr. Herbert Asquith and Messrs. Heinemann (publishers of *Pillicock Hill*, by Herbert Asquith) ; to the executors of the late Sir James Barrie, Frederick and Jelka Delius, and Sir Edward Elgar ; to Mrs. C. Elgar Blake ; and to *The Times*, *Punch*, *The Tatler and Bystander*, *The Birmingham Post* and *The Star*.

My thanks are due to Mr. Fred R. Gale for lending me a photograph of the Misses Bellingham's Preparatory School, Kensington, 1884 ; to *The Yorkshire Evening News* for the photograph taken at Harrogate in 1930 ; and to the Art Department of *The Times* for their invaluable assistance in preparing the illustrations.

Finally, for any omission in this list of acknowledgments, I should like sincerely to apologise to those concerned, and to assure them that no discourtesy has been intended.

D. H.

PORTRAIT OF A FRIEND

By

GEORGE BAKER

To attempt to write a portrait in words of Norman O'Neill
is a task of peculiar difficulty, even to an intimate friend like
myself, because many of the important and indeed essential
facets of his character were hidden from the public gaze.

Of course he was a charmer, everyone who came in contact
with him was aware of that. Tall, handsome, good figure,
wavy short grey hair, well groomed, pleasant smile, merry eyes,
well-modulated voice (tenor in pitch), cultured speech, courtly
manners, an infectious laugh—he was a millionaire in social
graces and held sway over the hearts of his friends and circles
far beyond with the ease of a jesting aristocrat.

But is this description of Norman the sum-total of the man?
By no means. The creator of the lovely music that poured
from his brain and pen with such apparent ease was something
far greater and finer than a mere debonair social charmer.

The clue to his more hidden characteristics is surely to be
found in his music, the half-elusive and delicate aromatic quality
of which is as hard to describe or define as that of his god, Delius.

The Norman that I and some of his other intimate friends
knew and loved so well was a sentimentalist who hated sentiment,
a diplomat who abhorred humbug, a man of affairs who found
commercialism distasteful, a genuine lover of music who was
allergic to Beethoven, a man of deep religious feeling with a
veneer of agnosticism, and, although he strongly disapproved
of lewd conversation, was at the same time a brilliant Rabelaisian
wit.

The truth about Norman is that he had a very sensitive
nature, and in order to protect himself from sudden waves of
emotion that threatened to overwhelm him he would often adopt
the attitude of a mocker and greet what we thought and hoped
were moving speeches with giggles, and sometimes ribald laughter.

Yes, he was a strange mixture. I can see and hear him now in
the Savage Club doing his impish best to shock the somewhat
humourless and gigantic figure of a man, the late Aubrey
Hammond, with Rabelaisian extravagancies, to the great
delight of his fellow-members. The same Norman (or was it
the hidden Norman?) was with me one day in the Club during

9

the last few weeks in the life of that distinguished writer and grand fellow, Basil Macdonald Hastings. Hastings, who was in the same room, knew that his own days were numbered, but there he was, putting up a brave show to his friends with his pungent witticisms and genial camaraderie. I remarked upon the magnificence of Mac's courage, whereupon Norman, who was visibly affected, said quietly, " It is the power of Jesus Christ."

Truer words could not have been uttered, for Macdonald Hastings was a member of an old Roman Catholic family, and he awaited his end with Christian fortitude.

This was the real Norman, the one I knew and loved. I speak what is in my heart when I say that of all my many departed Brother Savage companions there is none I miss more than the great artist, the merry-eyed charmer and the staunch friend—Norman O'Neill.

GEORGE BAKER.

NORMAN O'NEILL

A LIFE OF MUSIC

CHAPTER I

FAMILY HISTORY

THE first chapter of a biography is greatly assisted by some interesting ancestors. Norman O'Neill had an almost embarrassing number of them. He was a remarkable example of inherited talent, which came especially from his mother's side.

His great-grandfather, Arthur O'Neill, was a manufacturer of gold and silver watch-cases in the city of Dublin, at a time when the making of watch-cases, with its attendant chasing and engraving, was one of the fine arts. He seems to have been prosperous, for he owned a private house in Hoey's Court and a country cottage facing the green at Harold's Cross ; but by the end of his life the boom in watch-cases—like Dublin trade in general—was on the decline, and when his son Bernard, a clerk in the Board of Ordnance at Dublin Castle, tried to carry on the factory in his spare time for the benefit of his mother and sisters, he found the task too much for him. In the winding-up of the business, Bernard O'Neill was saddled with a load of debt which was to prove a constant source of anxiety. His salary was small, and by his marriage in 1815 to Sarah Gower, daughter of a Dublin solicitor, he had fifteen children. The ninth of these, born in 1828, was Norman's father, George Bernard O'Neill.

In 1837 the staff of Dublin Ordnance Office was cut down and Bernard O'Neill was among those threatened with a pension. Luckily, he had a friend at Court in London who had sufficient influence with the Master-General of the Ordnance to procure him the appointment of storekeeper in the carriage department at Woolwich. This proved a turning-point in the family history. The new storekeeper hurried over to Woolwich to find a suitable home, and his wife and children, travelling more sedately, joined him after a five days' voyage round Land's End.

Arriving in England at the age of nine, G. B. O'Neill went first to a school in Rectory Place, Woolwich, and then to another on the Common, where General Gordon was a schoolfellow. Soon he began to study art at the Royal Academy schools, winning the Gold Medal and other medals ; when he was nineteen his first picture was hung in the Academy, and from 1851 he exhibited annually.

A little notebook, recording " G. B's " income and expenses for nearly thirty years, is still in existence. From it we know that in 1851 he made £50, and in 1852 £150, while in 1853 he jumped to a higher level by earning £525. Having acquired an excellent general technique, he was already specialising in genre painting—a popular and profitable form of art in Victorian days—and the chief success of that year was represented by £63 " received from Mr. Colls for picture of ' Excursionists '." Two of the pictures that made his name were " The Foundling," later acquired by the Tate Gallery, and " The Obstinate Jury-man." Yet his total income for 1854 was barely £400, and the next year it was below £300. A less sturdy character might have hesitated before the responsibilities of matrimony, but " G. B." felt that, despite temporary reverses, he was fairly established in his profession, and at about the age of twenty-seven he married Emma Stuart Callcott, who was ten years younger than himself.

With this marriage a set of new traditions, the heritage of a talented family, was grafted on to the history of the O'Neills, and the influences affecting Norman O'Neill particularly declare themselves. Miss Callcott's father was William Hutchins Callcott (1807–1882), the composer and arranger, and her grandfather, Dr. John Wall Callcott (1766–1821), was a still more eminent musician, who ranked as one of the ablest composers of his day. Dr. Callcott is best remembered for his glee writing, and to a certain extent for his church music. Though he was taught by Haydn during his visit to England in 1791, he never had much skill in orchestral composition. He toiled ceaselessly on various literary works and lost his health because of them ; his musical grammar was published, but he never finished his musical dictionary, the material for which is now in the British Museum.

Dr. Callcott's brother—Emma's great-uncle—was Sir Augustus Wall Callcott, R.A. (1779–1844), the landscape painter, whose second wife wrote *Little Arthur's History of England*. Both men were handsome, Sir Augustus being called " the handsomest young man in Kensington," and Dr. Callcott's daughters were all good-looking. Basing their affections on the two old houses in the Mall where they were born, the brothers were staunch

Kensingtonians. A less likely volunteer than the learned Doctor could hardly be imagined, but he accepted a commission in the Kensington Volunteers when that corps was started in 1795, and formed a band for them, not only buying the instruments and composing the music but also teaching the members how to play.

Emma Callcott had other interesting, but more remote, connexions, through the marriage of her father's sister Betsy to William Horsley, another distinguished musician, who edited Dr. Callcott's best glees, catches and canons in two folio volumes. The eldest daughter of that couple married the great engineer Isambard Brunel, and one of the sons was J. C. Horsley, R.A., father of Sir Victor Horsley, the surgeon. Two other daughters, Fanny and Sophy, whose lively and interesting letters to their aunt Lucy Callcott have been published by Mrs. R. B. Gotch, were great friends of Mendelssohn on his frequent visits to England. There is no doubt that music was the controlling influence in Emma's family.

Perhaps the best evidence of the success of Miss Callcott's marriage is provided in her husband's little cash-book. The yearly totals now took a higher trend, so that by 1857 the painter's annual " net profit " was over seven hundred pounds. The pair started their married life at the Mall, but in 1863 were sufficiently prosperous, by Victorian standards, to rent a home of their own in the country. The choice fell on Willesley, a lovely fifteenth-century house about a mile from Cranbrook, Kent, on the main road to Maidstone.

Girls came first of the six children : Constance (who married Cecil Benson, brother of Sir Frank Benson and Lord Charnwood); Kathleen, who died in her early thirties ; and Alice, who died still younger. Then came the boys : Harry, Frank and Norman. But before Norman was born, his father possessed a home in London as well as in the country. In 1873 he took the house with the bow windows in Young Street, Kensington, and set up his easel in the room in which Thackeray had written *Vanity Fair*, *Pendennis*, and *Esmond*.

CHAPTER II

CHILDHOOD AND BOYHOOD

NORMAN HOUSTOUN O'NEILL—he owed his Christian names to his godfathers, Norman Shaw, R.A., and Admiral Wallace Houstoun, old friends of his father—was born at 16 (formerly 13) Young Street on March 14, 1875. A bright, cheerful little boy, he soon showed signs of the happy temperament which was to be his throughout life ; but he was very delicate, and until the age of twelve spent miserable winters, with constant attacks of croup. It was thought risky to send him away to boarding-school, and he was taught at home and at various private schools in Kensington.

Norman, of course, knew a Kensington of charm and dignity that has long since vanished, presumably for ever. He remembered the days when John Barker, who started business as a small draper, enlarged his shop to deal with groceries, and the old-established provision merchant next door displayed a notice in his window, saying, " Beware of Cream sold by Drapers ! " For a time he went to the Misses Bellingham's dame school in Scarsdale Villas. With his long wavy hair and already charming features, Norman is certainly the most handsome, and probably the most intelligent-looking, of the little boys in a school group taken when he was nine, and the photograph (reproduced on another page) lends point to a remark of one of his contemporaries, that " even as a child Norman used to look like a celebrity." In his Scarsdale Villas days he had a fondness for making pencil drawings on an heroic scale, which necessitated the buying of paper by the roll from the local stationer.

For the first ten years of his life, however, Norman spent as much of his time at Willesley as in Kensington. Cranbrook was then the centre of a colony of artists, members of " the British school," who specialised in genre painting of domestic subjects. The doyen was old Tom Webster, R.A., whose pictures of boys' schools and games were once to be found reproduced in nearly every hotel in England. Others, beside G. B. O'Neill, were his cousin, J. C. Horsley, and his son, Walter, and the brothers F. D. and George Hardy. Tom Webster was a great figure in Cranbrook—with long white hair falling over his black velvet coat, he drove along the country lanes in a bath chair pulled by a donkey. Another memorable sight for Norman to meet on his walks was the local rat-catcher, an Arabian-Nights figure with silky black curls, who was drawn by four goats in a kind of child's trolley, on which he squatted with immobile features.

These were the celebrities of Cranbrook in the eighteen-eighties. Norman, in his impressionable years, was certainly influenced by what he saw of them, and by his artistic surroundings at Willesley. Even to the children the lovely panelled walls and oak floors and beams of the house were a joy. "G. B." had the connoisseur's eye for a good piece of furniture. The most astonishing of his bargains was an old *petit-point* chair which figured in many of his interiors ; this was bought for £5, and, on his death, after fifty years' service, was sold at Christie's for 575 guineas.

When Norman was born, his father was enjoying the most lucrative period of his career. In the year 1875, according to the little notebook, he made £1335, and in 1876 " Our Boys," one of his most popular pictures, which showed Mrs. O'Neill seated on the *petit-point* chair with Norman in her arms and his two elder brothers beside her, was bought by Admiral Houstoun for £350. All the children had to sit for their father in turn, and usually disliked it, despite the accruing sixpences. A great Academy success was " Gee-up," a girl carrying a little boy pick-a-back, with the stone mounting-steps of Willesley in the background. Norman was the boy, and the girl was his sister Constance. " Consie " was a lovely girl, and, like her mother, what is known as " a Burne-Jones type " ; in fact, she sat for Burne-Jones as one of the girls in his picture, " The Golden Stair." As often with his most successful works, O'Neill painted a replica of " Gee-up." He called it " Pick-a-back," and it is reproduced in this book.

" Our Boys," " Gee-up," " Spare the Weeds," and many other examples of G. B. O'Neill's work were popularised in engravings and in the fashionable but detestable oleographs of the period. Enough has been said of his style to show that it did not aspire to originality, indeed the very titles of his pictures are sufficient to tell us that they were " typically Victorian." But even in those days pictures did not sell for three or four hundred pounds without possessing genuine merit ; in O'Neill's case this was to be found in sensitive colouring and composition, careful and accurate detail. His pictures lose considerably in reproduction. Seen face to face, the best of them have something of the effect of a mellow " set " on the stage, designed by a producer who knows how to use stage lighting.

The Cranbrook years were happy for Norman.   Probably they not only implanted in him a love of the countryside but also—what was much less to be expected—a love of the theatre. G. B. O'Neill was a keen theatre-goer, and at Willesley home-made plays and charades, in which from an early age Norman took part, were the fashion.   For one memorable performance Frank O'Neill played the part of a mother surrounded by several babies—who consisted of Norman and a lot of dolls.   The husband (their elder brother Harry) was supposed to have just returned from long travels abroad, and when he had finished a stirring account of his adventures, the " mother " quietly pointed to her young family and said, " I too have not been idle ! "—a remark which, to the actors' astonishment, brought the house down.

Cricket flourished in the Willesley orchard ; the trees round the wicket were set like fieldsmen, and if you hit them full pitch you were out, caught.   Harry and Frank each batted eleven times, and when Norman was old enough he was allowed to bat for " extras."   But games never had a great hold on him.   Nature was his first and abiding love, and he saw the orchard with other than a sportsman's eye.   At the age of eight he was found to have buried a field-mouse in one corner of it, and written this epitaph on a piece of paper :

> Here lies a filled mous
> Found on the frunt lawn
> At Old Willesley.
> Very small.
> A dere animal too
> Small and weak.
> A cat i think did do it
> He new no better.

And here is a little story, written about the same time, which shows that he early possessed a sense of the dramatic :

One day a little fishing boat sald in the sea, the waves were still.   Now think how waves ror in the knight.   i will tell you, my friends.   One dark dark knight they had only cort 24 little fishes.   The litning was dreful and 8 men were gorn.   O.O. crite the men—dear dear—our best men.   The thunder was offul and bad.   the waves were hie.   O such fome.   Al off a sudden a flack of litning came and the man was dached away.   the spars were gorn and you know wen the spars are gorn the men can't take hold off them.   then only 1 mast was left and the storm went on.

O.O. crid the men, as the skiper was washed away and one man went after him and he and the skiper were dround and the last mast went.   I am shur that a fisherman's life is a hard one and they don't get much money.

I.—NORMAN BEING CARRIED BY HIS SISTER CONSIE
(Later Mrs. Cecil Benson), with the old mounting-steps at Willesley
in the background.

II.—NORMAN, AGED NINE

(*Centre, back row*), at the Misses Bellingham's preparatory school, Scarsdale Villas, Kensington, in 1884.

In 1886 Willesley was given up. For the next six years the house in Young Street was the centre of Norman's existence. He was brought up to attend church regularly, and became a choir-boy at St. Mary Abbot's. There was a moment when it was thought that a naval career would be of great benefit to his health, and Norman was by no means opposed to an idea which, of course, had the warm support of Admiral Houstoun ; but he had already shown that genuine aptitude for music which will not be denied expression. He started learning the piano when he was six, and at ten he composed a small sonata, which he dedicated to his mother ; it is not original, but has a distinct Mozartian flavour, neat in shape, coherent and melodious.

Kensington Square in those days was a centre of culture and the arts, and the O'Neills, whose house stood just round the corner, profited greatly from the interesting society to be found there. Dr. John Merriman, who looked after the Teck and Argyll families at Kensington Palace and brought Queen Mary into the world ; Kegan Paul, the publisher ; Arthur Somervell and Hubert Parry, the musicians,—all lived in the Square and were their friends, as were Thackeray's daughter, Mrs. Richmond Ritchie, and J. W. Mackail, who lived opposite them in Young Street. Dr. Merriman's grandson, Paget Bowman, was Norman's closest friend. He always cherished memories of holidays spent with the Bowmans at Joldwynds, Holmbury St. Mary (where he first met Ralph Vaughan Williams, watching a village cricket match), and with the Cazalet family at Greenhurst, Capel. These visits gave him a lasting affection for the Surrey hills.

Their father often took the O'Neill boys to theatres, and sometimes to the smoking concerts given by a Mr. Plater of Kensington, who provided an excellent male-voice quartet which introduced them to the glees of their great-grandfather and of William Horsley. Other red-letter days were those on which the members of the Etching Club (of which " G. B." was a founder) met at 16 Young Street to compare specimens of their work. These were like first-nights at the theatre for the boys, who hid on the stairs to watch the visitors arrive, not perhaps such distinguished visitors as those who had walked through the same front-door on the famous evening when Thackeray gave his party for Charlotte Brontë, but still an interesting collection, which included many of the leading artists of the day. There were also regular visits to Norman's godfather, Norman Shaw, the architect (whose life has been well and deservedly written by Sir Reginald Blomfield). Shaw lived at Hampstead.

One of Norman's early memories was of leaving the underground at its then terminus of Swiss Cottage and walking through the open fields to his house.

Mrs. O'Neill was particularly devoted to the youngest and most delicate of her sons ; the home atmosphere was encouraging and stimulating for a boy of artistic temperament. As a painter, " G. B." kept to the domestic subjects which he could do best, but he was interested in the modernists, visited their studios, and admired the teaching of Morris and Ruskin. The illustrations of Kate Greenaway, Randolph Caldecott, and Walter Crane—the Cranes were neighbours in Holland Street whose parties were remembered—gave much enjoyment in the Young Street nursery.

A chance meeting brought Norman to the fringe of a different artistic world. In May 1891, travelling to Piccadilly on the top of a horse bus, he found himself next to a well-known Kensington figure—a Russian poet, dreamer and litterateur, who spoke many languages and was the friend of many artists—Count Eric Stenbock. Stenbock was delighted with his intelligence, and the acquaintance ripened. Through Stenbock he came to know the work of Conder and the writings of Wilde, and to meet Aubrey Beardsley, who was only three years older than himself.

Since he was fourteen, Norman had been having lessons in theory and composition from his father's neighbour, Dr. (afterwards Sir) Arthur Somervell, who thought him highly promising, and who years later was to write : " Although our paths in life did not bring us much together, my heart always leaped when I saw him, and our friendship seemed untouched by long separations." Others of his parents' friends who did much to encourage him in those early days were J. A. Fuller-Maitland (for many years music critic of *The Times*) and that first-class musician and accompanist, Henry Bird. Fuller-Maitland wrote wisely to Mrs. O'Neill :

There is no possible doubt that your son has very remarkable abilities, and gives very decided promise that he will not disgrace his illustrious ancestors. His playing is wonderfully intelligent, and will always be delightful to listen to, though I doubt, as I told him, his being able to make enough progress to take a very high position as a public player, and it will not do for him to take any but a high position, whatever he does. His composition strikes me as being the more remarkable of the two. . . .

With Bird, Norman began rather reluctantly to study the organ. It was generally thought in those days that the best way for an Englishman to earn a living in music was to become an

organist.   But the "king of instruments" never appealed to
him, and he was fortunate to be introduced by the Horsleys to
Joseph Joachim, and to be able to show him some of his early
efforts in composition.   Joachim agreed that he was distinctly
gifted, and suggested that he should be sent to Frankfort-on-
Main to study composition with Professor Iwan Knorr.

CHAPTER III

FRANKFORT STUDENT

NORMAN O'NEILL came to Frankfort as a student at the Hoch Conservatorium in 1893, and made rapid progress under the tuition of Iwan Knorr, a Russianised German composer who (to use Norman's own words) had ".a positive genius for imparting the technique of composition." The musical education offered in Frankfort at that time was second to none, and Norman was particularly fortunate in his fellow-students, who from time to time included Balfour Gardiner, Percy Grainger, Roger Quilter and Cyril Scott. They learned a good deal from each other, and were later called "the Frankfort gang" by some of their fellow-composers. Of the four, Gardiner was nearest to Norman in age ; Cyril Scott, a boy prodigy, was then only fourteen (he returned to England for a time to further his education) ; and in 1893 Percy Grainger was a striking-looking lad of ten with a mass of curly golden hair. Other of Norman's friends at Frankfort were Thomas Holland-Smith (who eventually taught at Durham School) ; Herbert Golden, later taken on to the teaching staff of the Hoch Conservatorium ; Carlo Fischer and Henry Purmort Eames, both of whom made their mark in the musical life of the United States, in Minneapolis and California respectively ; and one to whom he was particularly devoted—Clemens von Franckenstein, who became "Intendant" of the Munich opera and was a brother of the former Austrian Ambassador in London, Sir George Franckenstein.

Count Stenbock still kept a friendly eye on his protégé. He wrote to Norman in his early days at Frankfort :

. . . I meant, like Tacitus, to lecture you "De Germaniâ" wh. I now will proceed to do. In *learning* at first it is better to listen to people talking than to read much—but it is a particularly good thing to read all the advertisements on the walls, especially the more familiar ones, *e.g.* "Lieber Herr Pears, seit dem ich Ihre Seife einmal gebraucht, habe ich keine andere brauchen können—Adeline Patti." Thus you get gradually almost instinctively to know the order of the construction of sentences, wherein German always seems so alien. But whatever you do, avoid colloquialism—you know how awful a foreigner sounds talking English slang—and in your part of Germany quite respectable people leave out the "n's" from words ending in "en" and the final " e " from words ending in " e," not to speak of their vulgar pronunciation, making " ai " and " ei " just the same, also " eu," " äu," and " oi " all alike. Remember Germany is not England, and education (really public there) is much more widely diffused ; so you always take off your hat in a shop—also the gentleman greets the lady first—also the hat must be taken off quite (even small schoolboys take off their hats to one another). The beer is good and harmless ; don't be afraid of the black beer, it is not porter. The cheap white wines are very good, but beware of the red. . . .

The advice was sound, and Norman may have benefited from it, for he spoke German excellently all his life ; it is doubtful whether he needed to be reminded to " take the hat off quite," for his manners were always perfect. At about the same time Stenbock persuaded Aubrey Beardsley to do some impressions of " the English flower in the German conservatory " which were sent out to Norman with Stenbock's captions, and with Beardsley's signature on a covering note. Three of these typical and hitherto unpublished Beardsley sketches are reproduced in these pages ; a fourth was of Norman, masked, fighting a duel. They show that Beardsley knew his subject well enough to get a good likeness, and to convey a vivid idea of a spirited young man.

Stenbock wrote often and Norman kept all his letters, which were full of humour. Like other foreigners, the Count was fond of joking about Queen Victoria, and once he wrote of her :

> This is a thing which no one knows
> How the Queen looks without her clothes :
> Even Companions of the Bath
> Know not the form our good Queen hath !

But Stenbock was a sick man who, though he had moods of gaiety, was more often melancholy and depressed. To Norman he gave a Kelmscott copy of Lady Wilde's translation of *Sidonia, the Sorceress,* and a rare illustrated edition of Blake's *Songs of Experience,* beside his own poems ; but Norman owed still more to this forgotten figure of the 'nineties, for after his death in April 1895 (at the age of thirty-five) Stenbock was found to have left him £1500 to assist his musical studies, which meant that Norman could afford a valuable final year at the Conservatoire.

At the beginning of his stay in Frankfort, Norman had a few lessons from Engelbert Humperdinck. The composer of *Hansel and Gretel* was not a satisfactory teacher. According to Cyril Scott, in *My Years of Indiscretion,* he " used to keep O'Neill and his friend Holland-Smith waiting twenty minutes before he remembered to enter the classroom at all—and then, having arrived and listened to them a bit, would disappear, never to return." Humperdinck's exits appear to have been as silent as they were abrupt. " I would be labouring at some complicated score," Holland-Smith told Scott, "when suddenly I would hear Norman O'Neill giggling behind me. Rather annoyed at him for ridiculing my miserable efforts, I would turn round. 'You needn't bother to keep that up,' said the culprit, 'he's gone. . . .'"

Holland-Smith and Norman lodged together and had great fun cooking English breakfasts on a German stove which was always going out. Balfour Gardiner entered the Conservatorium in October 1894. "Norman came to call on me," writes Mr. Gardiner, "and made a great impression. He talked neither of cricket nor football; he was, like myself, intensely interested in music (his own music was very English); and he had a charm of manner that he retained till the end of his life. We became close friends." Norman and Balfour Gardiner were both piano pupils of an Italian called Uzielli.

While Norman's humour and gaiety made him popular with other young men, his charming smile and distinguished, aristocratic appearance were not without effect on the opposite sex. He had with him an air of "not caring"—not exactly a pose but a kind of detachment,—which veiled a deeply sensitive and emotional nature. Already Knorr must have noticed that he had also that clear, tidy mind, coupled with great musicality, which go to the making of a good teacher; for he soon recommended him to a young English student, Edith Meadows, as a suitable person to give her harmony lessons for a modest fee.

Norman came to teach Miss Meadows harmony at the pension in which she was staying with her friend Adine Ruckert, who had been brought up in Paris and had won a medal at the Paris Conservatoire. Both girls were in Frankfort to have piano lessons from Madame Clara Schumann, the famous teacher and widow of the composer. Norman and Adine Ruckert had noticed each other at the symphony concerts before they actually met on the long staircase leading to the flat where the girls lodged, when Norman discovered that Adine was not only pretty but more than usually intelligent. A friendship rapidly sprang up between these two. Adine abandoned her harmony lessons with a German professor who knew neither English nor French, and in the autumn of 1895 she became Norman's second pupil.

Those Frankfort days were enchanting, and they were not to be forgotten. First-class music was provided at the Opera and at the concerts of the Museumsgesellschaft, and it was a wonderful experience for young students to hear Joachim playing the Brahms violin concerto, with Brahms and Clara Schumann sitting in the front row of the stalls ; to see Richard Strauss conduct first performances of his works ; or to hear (as Adine did) the first performances of the two sonatas for piano and clarinet Brahms composed for Muhlfeld, played from manuscript in Clara Schumann's salon by the great clarinetist and the composer himself. At the other end of the scale were the delights of wine taverns and cafés and expeditions into the Taunus mountains ; while Norman, in the gallery at the Opera, could laugh so loud at certain shapeless Wagnerian singers and the sounds they produced, that he and his friends were often threatened with expulsion.

The tuition which he gave Adine was certainly harmonious, even if not much harmony was learnt. At the end of the lessons the couple often had tea together. They had plenty to talk about, for Norman knew little of French music and painting, while Adine was equally ignorant of English art and literature ; Norman read her the poems of Keats, Shelley, Swinburne and other favourites. Adine Ruckert's father had been Swiss, a descendant of a well-known family of harpsichord makers. Her grandmother came from Vannes, in Brittany ; her mother from Paris. The latter had been left a widow with two daughters and had married as her second husband a director of an important firm of rice merchants, M. Adolphe Philippi, who, after living for some years in London, retired from business and took a large house in Neuilly, near Paris.

These and many other details of their respective families and ways of life were exchanged during the next few months, and before long the couple found themselves very much in love. An idyllic existence came to an end with the death of Madame Schumann in May 1896. Adine attended the beautiful funeral service at her house, when pupils from Stockhausen's vocal school sang ; but her parents could see no reason why she should continue to stay in Frankfort, and after a few weeks she left reluctantly for Paris. The harmony lessons had never got as far as counterpoint. At the last lesson, when Adine offered the fee as usual, Norman refused to take it and the money went all over the floor. From this time they considered themselves engaged to be married.

This early engagement (Norman had just passed his twenty-first birthday) was a serious step which Norman worked hard to justify in the eyes of his own and Adine's parents. He had already begun to compose, and a group of songs performed at one of the Conservatorium concerts in March 1896 provided him with the first of many newspaper cuttings : a short criticism sent by a Frankfort correspondent to the *Musical Courier* and later copied into the *Musical Times*. " Each of the group is worthy of the master of this student," it said ; " they are tuneful, fully and beautifully worked out in all parts, and finished in polished style. This young man has something to say in the world of tone, and he is saying it forcibly and sympathetically, and will before long speak to more of the world, in higher planes, no doubt."

Two of these songs eventually found a publisher. " Parted," the first music by Norman to be published, was written to words by his brother Frank, and was printed by Weekes in 1897 ; " Norse Lullaby," a setting of Eugene Field's poem, was published by Boosey in 1898. But in the meantime Norman was trying his hand at more ambitious works. A delightful trio for piano, violin and 'cello (variations on the old folk-tune, " Pretty Polly Oliver "), and a sonata for piano and 'cello were both given their first performances in Frankfort. He began to orchestrate, practised his piano-playing, and toiled at " form " and " fugues."

Norman and Adine contrived to see each other about every three months, either in London, in Paris, or on holidays elsewhere on the Continent. His first meeting with Adine's parents was at the Black Forest village of Gernsbach in the Murgtal in August 1896. M. and Mme Philippi naturally approached the interview with some doubt—not to say anxiety,—but they were agreeably surprised by their daughter's young musician and, like everyone else, soon fell under his charm. Adine and Norman were both thrilled when, after a few days, M. Philippi introduced him to an English visitor, in the garden of the Hotel Pfeiffer, as " Norman O'Neill, my future son-in-law ! " The O'Neill family in London received Adine equally kindly.

Norman's last year in Frankfort, 1896–7, was a year of steady work. He lived, as always, most economically, part of Count Stenbock's legacy being allotted to each month. At the beginning of the month life was fairly affluent, but as time went on meals had to be taken in cheaper and still cheaper restaurants, until by the end of the month he was sometimes subsisting on sandwiches. Cyril Scott, now showing a most prolific and original talent, returned to Frankfort in the autumn of 1896 ; through him Norman came to know the poet Stefan George, with whom they went on a bicycle expedition ; but the year was chiefly memorable for the beginning of his friendship with Clemens von Franckenstein, who had lately arrived from Munich. In September 1897 Norman settled down again with his parents in Kensington, determined to move heaven and earth (but especially earth) to make a living in music that would enable him to marry in two years' time.

CHAPTER IV

EARNING A LIVING

THE O'Neills had left Thackeray's house in Young Street by the time that Norman's student days were over, and he began his career as a professional musician at their new home, 18 Victoria Road, close by. Long afterwards he wrote an article for a musical paper, in which he said :

> I returned to London full of hopes, and above all anxious to get my immortal works, as I thought them, published, played and performed. I was soon to find this was no easy matter. One had been rather spoiled in Frankfort, where no sooner was a piece finished that it was played at one of the Conservatorium concerts.
> "How was one to earn a living ? I now regretted my contempt for the organ ! I could play the piano passably, but was not a solo-pianist, and like many such thought I could teach it. Harmony and composition ? Yes—if I could find the pupils. Or if I could manage to write a successful song that might help to keep the wolf from the door, and give me time to work at the ambitious things I had in mind. But the training I had been through was a very serious one, and I found it almost impossible to write light, and what was termed attractive music. . . .

The sense in which Norman used the word " impossible " is shown in a passage from a letter he wrote to Adine on October 27, 1897 : " I *can* write bad, and even music for the *un*musical, if I like ! But I do *not* ' like,' though it is a temptation when one sees how a reputation, if one can call it such, can easily be made by a musical person of average brains ! "

He went out a lot, to concerts and musical " at homes," so as to meet people who might be able to give him a helping hand. At the house of that kindly old musician, Wilhelm Ganz (whose son Albert became a life-long friend), he met Alfred Kalisch, the music critic, who was reader for Forsyth Brothers, and Kalisch was helpful in having four pieces for piano published, at the beginning of 1898, in a green cover with shamrocks designed by Norman's sister Kathleen. It was at the Ganzs', too, that he met the singer Gregory Hast, who gave to the public, a year or two later, Norman's lovely songs, " Roses in the Garden " and " When Passion's Trance." Fuller-Maitland was another who was always willing to provide introductions ; as a result of two of these, Plunket Greene sang Norman's setting of Hartley Coleridge's " The Light of Love " (published in 1899), and

Evangeline Florence often included in her programmes the " Norse Lullaby."

The letter to Adine which has just been quoted contained a description of Norman's first meeting, at a party the previous night, with the conductor Hans Richter :

> . . . Richter is quite charming—a nice fat simple old German ! After the ladies left the room I was talking to him for some time and his "keenness" on music is quite delightful, in a man who is nicht mehr jung. They made me play just before he was going, and he said to me as he took my hand, *patting* it with his other : " Ich hoffe bald wieder von Ihnen zu *hören* ! "

Gradually Norman's circle of musical friends widened. In 1898, through his sister Kathleen, he got to know that clever and humorous woman, Mrs. Rosa Newmarch, whose writings were then introducing the English public to the composers of the Russian school ; and through Mrs. Newmarch he met Henry Wood and his Russian wife, who charmed him by her singing of Russian songs. From the first, Wood was interested in Norman's compositions : " O'Neill's works," he says in *My Life of Music*, " have always appealed to me."

In course of time Norman succeeded in gathering a certain number of pupils for piano and harmony lessons. Old friends of the O'Neills were Mr. Maberly Smith, rector of Penshurst, Kent, and his wife, who invited Norman to organise a choir and conduct an amateur orchestra for them. For several years he used to go down to Penshurst regularly, staying the night at the rectory ; the experience was invaluable, and he enjoyed these visits, for the members of the " Penshurst Vocal and Instrumental Society " (with Lady Hardinge of Penshurst in the first violins, and the Hon. Lavinia Hardinge in the second violins) made up in keenness for what they lacked in numbers.

In January 1898, Dr. Scholz, the Director of the Frankfort Conservatorium, wrote to Norman to ask whether he would accept the post of " musical secretary " to the blind Landgrave of Hesse, a talented amateur musician, though a poor composer. Norman declined the honour, on the ground that he could not interrupt his career just when he was beginning to establish himself. In August of that year he stayed for a sunny holiday with Clemens von Franckenstein at the family chalet at Alt-Aussee in the Tyrol, sailing and swimming, and meeting Jacob Wassermann and other interesting people. He stopped at Frankfort on the way home to show Knorr an orchestral suite in four movements he had just completed ; it had a lovely slow movement, but Knorr was not satisfied with the last movement ; which Norman re-wrote. This suite was eventually sent to Professor Brodsky in Manchester, who showed it to Richter ; the latter thought it highly promising but not quite mature enough to appear in one of his programmes.

While Norman was busy in London, his fiancé was hard at work in Paris. Adine Ruckert had made up her mind to continue seriously with her music, so as to be able, by playing in public and teaching, to contribute her share to the joint income after marriage. It was not easy to find a successor to Madame Schumann, but eventually she decided to study with that remarkable Czech pianist, the wife of an exiled Hungarian author and journalist who had settled in Paris, Madame Wilhelmine Clauss-Szarvady. As a girl Madame Szarvady had played to Griepenkerl, a former pupil of Philip Emmanuel Bach ; when she was fourteen Schumann had heard her, and had been so impressed that he allowed her to play his Concerto from manuscript. Her playing was notable for its tone and for the fullness and mellowness of her touch. At the Paris Conservatoire Adine had learnt dexterity and clearness of execution ; with Madame Schumann she had studied the art of legato touch and much attention had been given to the quality of finger touch ; now, with Madame Szarvady, she learned a broader method of playing, which depended largely on the use of forearm and arm attack. Between Madame Szarvady and her pupils, " Colour ! " was always the watchword.

Adine soon showed not only that she was an outstanding pupil of outstanding teachers, but that her marriage was destined to be that rare thing, a true partnership in music. In the course of the year 1898 she learned two new compositions by her fiancé—a piano and violin sonata, and Variations and Fugue for piano on a theme written by herself. She went to Frankfort that winter to look up old friends and to introduce these works to them. She played the Variations to Knorr and Uzielli, who were greatly impressed, both by Norman's composition and by the quality of Adine's interpretation. The sonata she played with Hugo Herrmann and with Rehbner ; it was eventually reduced to the two middle movements, the best of the four, and became known as Scherzo and Romance (op. 6).

Her first public recital was given at the Salle Erard in Paris in February 1899. The programme included studies, preludes and the " Barcarolle " of Chopin, Schumann's " Carnaval," and Norman's new Variations and Fugue " On a theme by A. R."

(the first public performance). The recital was a great success, and the Variations were liked and obtained good notices in the French musical papers. Adine went to considerable trouble over these Variations. She played them to many eminent musicians and paid several visits, with letters of introduction, to Paris publishers, all of whom gave the same answer : " Too long—Too difficult—Can you play us some smaller pieces ? " Later, in London, Forsyth offered to publish them if Norman would pay £8 towards the cost ; but £8 meant a great deal in those days, and when he refused, their fate was sealed.

This was one of the works to which Norman gave the name of " Boomerangs," because they always returned so quickly. " Everywhere it was the same tale, ' There is no market for serious music,' "—Norman later wrote in an article : " and one could read between the lines, ' At any rate not for an unknown quantity like yourself.' "

However, a small income was now coming in ; Norman's songs had attracted some notice ; Adine's recital had been encouraging ; parents were kind ; and the couple decided that their marriage must not be postponed any longer. In May 1899 Adine and her mother came over to London to look for a suitable place for them to live in. As Norman was very fond of Kensington, and did not want to leave the home of his ancestors, they were lucky in finding vacant a charming little house, No. 7 Edwardes Square, at the moderate rent of £80 a year. M. and Madame Philippi furnished the house for them—a handsome wedding present.

Norman and Adine were married on July 12, 1899, first at the town-hall of Neuilly, and then at the small French Protestant church there. Important events could never quite subdue Norman's boyish spirit, and, while he and the family guests were waiting in Madame Philippi's drawing-room before the wedding, he kept playing with the two gold wedding-rings and throwing them up and down. One fell and rolled under a piece of furniture. When Adine arrived, in all dignity, with her white veil and long train, she discovered the wedding party on hands and knees, searching everywhere. The ring was found at last, but the delay made them late. Worse awaited them at the town-hall, where M. le Maire, a pompous figure with the tricolour sash covering his imposing corporation, began the proceedings by solemnly intoning " Norman Houstoun O'Neill " in the French phonetic pronunciation. Norman was overcome and they both found it difficult to stop giggling.

The bridegroom's mother was at the wedding, and Paget Bowman acted as his best man. An old friend of Adine's at the Paris Conservatoire, Henri Busser, the composer and conductor (later Director of the Paris Opera), played the organ at the church service. At five o'clock in the afternoon Mr. and Mrs. Norman O'Neill left Paris on the Basle express for a month's honeymoon in the Black Forest.

CHAPTER V

MARTIN-HARVEY AND THE " PROMS "

THE house in Edwardes Square, with its outlook on the well-kept square garden, was easily run and proved ideal for a newly married couple. Norman made one of the top-floor rooms into a studio and worked at an upright Broadwood on chamber music, orchestral works and songs. He gave piano and harmony lessons and went regularly to Penshurst ; he also taught at a girls' school at Highgate—this he particularly hated, for the rooms were cold, the girls had chilblains, and an uneatable lunch was brought to him on a tray. In money matters he soon showed a keen sense of responsibility which never deserted him. Physically he was much stronger ; his looks were the more striking for the contrast between prematurely grey hair and features that remained youthful to the end.

Adine also began to give private lessons, and to introduce some of Norman's works at public concerts. Their first joint ventures in this line were two chamber music concerts given at the Steinway Hall in November and December 1900. At the first of these a new trio of Norman's, for piano, violin and 'cello, in A minor (op. 7) was given ; at the second, the Variations and Fugue which had already been heard in Paris. Some of Norman's early work had shown the influence of Brahms, but he was now writing music that was generally recognised as original and distinctive. The critic of *The Star* said :—

Mr. Norman O'Neill has studied in Germany, but he has had the good sense—or good fortune—or both—to bring back with him from there only what is good. He has left behind the mistiness, the desire to say everything at the greatest possible length, and the contempt for anything that sounds agreeable, which seems to be the chief equipment of many who go to Germany. The Trio shows Mr. O'Neill to have an excellent sense of proportion and balance, a keen appreciation of the virtue of conciseness, besides a considerable gift of inventing melodies. His themes have the great merit of moving on—not stopping as though short of breath. . . . The whole work is extremely attractive and expressive. . . .

A year later the London critics were unanimous in their approval of Norman's first important orchestral work, the overture " In Autumn," which was dedicated to Henry Wood and given its first performance by him in October 1901 at a Promenade Concert at the Queen's Hall. " On Saturday," said

The Times of October 28, " the legend ' first time ' was affixed
to two works. Of these, the more important in size was a suite
of incidental music by M. Jean Sibelius, a Finn, to Adolf Paul's
comedy, *King Christian II.* But the musical interest was in inverse
ratio to the size, for Mr. Norman O'Neill's overture, ' In Autumn,'
was incomparably more delightful to hear. There is nothing
in it of the sere and yellow leaf of autumn, but rather the cheerfulness of a summer evening, while the picture, whatever it may
be, is depicted with a delicate yet masterly touch, and freshness
and grace are over it all." *The Observer* declared that it was " a
work that warrants high hopes for this young composer's future,"
and other critics took up the chorus of praise with " eminently
poetical," " as important a piece as any Mr. Wood has given
us this season," " exceptional abilities," and so forth. " In
Autumn " was played soon afterwards by Richter at one of the
Gentlemen's Concerts in Manchester. A Birmingham audience
was delighted with the overture when it was given by the Halford
Society.

These performances of " In Autumn " were followed by many
others in provincial towns, but did not, as Norman had hoped,
lead to its publication. " As one had to copy the parts oneself,
often a matter of weeks of drudgery when more than one set
was required, or bear the expenses of having them copied out
of one's slender resources, there was not much more than honour
and glory resulting ! " he wrote in an article, long afterwards.

The year 1901 was important in Norman's life not only for
the success of his concert overture but also because it marked the
beginning of his long association with the stage. This was
indirectly due to a visit paid in that year by Mr. and Mrs. John
Martin-Harvey to East Preston, where Norman's brother Frank
was then engaged (as Martin-Harvey says in his *Autobiography*)
in " coaching . . . growing grapes, and breeding ' wire-hairs.' "
A chance meeting led to Frank O'Neill's acceptance of Martin-
Harvey's proposal that he should become his business manager,
and he began work on the second tour of *The Only Way*, in the
course of which Martin-Harvey intended to produce, at Dublin,
a version of Lytton's *Eugene Aram* called *After All*. Incidental
music was needed for *After All*, which was coming to the Avenue
Theatre, London, after Christmas, and Frank suggested that
his brother would be the right man to compose it. Norman
wrote a song with harp accompaniment for Mabel Terry-Lewis
(published by Boosey) and a delightful little " song of welcome "
for the village children to sing at Aram's wedding.

The English Flower in the German Conservatory

III.—THE ENGLISH FLOWER IN THE GERMAN CONSERVATORY

Aubrey Beardsley's impression of Norman O'Neill, at about eighteen, in his early days at the Frankfort Conservatorium.

IV.—" N. BEGS FROM MAYOR PERMISSION TO PLAY GOLF," and " N. THE MASHER"

Other sketches of Norman O'Neill by Aubrey Beardsley, now first published ; the writing is that of Count Stenbock who forwarded them to Frankfort.

Henceforth Martin-Harvey remembered him whenever he had a play that called for music. Norman's second commission was for *The Exile*, an unsuccessful piece by Lloyd Osbourne and Austin Strong, in which Martin-Harvey as Napoleon had to drill the children of St. Helena outside his prison house. For this pathetic moment Norman composed a charming little march, but at rehearsal Martin-Harvey jumped up and said, " This wants the Marseillaise ! " Out crashed Rouget de L'Isle's magnificent tune, but somehow friendly critics in the stalls were not impressed ; the music overpowered the pathos ; and back, triumphantly, went Norman's march.

Martin-Harvey's commissions were, of course, few and far between, and during the early years of the century Norman's chief energies were given to orchestral and chamber music. In these years Adine fulfilled many engagements up and down the country, playing in Manchester with the Brodsky quartet, at Balliol College, Oxford, at Birmingham and elsewhere. A chamber music concert which she gave at the Steinway Hall in February 1903 was entirely made up of works by Norman, including the first performance of his piano quintet in E minor (op. 10) ; Edith Clegg and Leonhard Sickert sang several new songs, among them two with words by Mrs. Newmarch, and settings of Shelley's " The Indian Serenade " and Verlaine's " Un grand sommeil noir " ; and the programme ended with the " Pretty Polly Oliver " variations, " an earlier work," as *The Times* said, " but none the less successful." Adine played the quintet again, with the Kruse quartet, later in the year, at one of the Saturday " Pops."

Another work of Norman's that must be mentioned here is his Ballade for contralto and orchestra, " Death on the hills," sung by Miss Grainger Kerr at a promenade concert in 1904. This was a setting of a somewhat gruesome poem translated from the Russian by Mrs. Newmarch and probably the subject did not make for a wide popularity. " Mr. O'Neill seems bent, like the Fat Boy in *Pickwick*, on ' making your flesh creep,' " said one critic, " and succeeds only too effectually." But there was general recognition of the unconventional thematic material and able scoring in the work.

The joint musical life was full and varied. Norman edited the first volume of Boosey's *Golden Treasury of Song* (1903), which contained fifty songs by famous composers from Arne to Wagner (the selection was admirable and the keys most suitable for general use) ; and in 1906 Arnold published his charming *Song-Garden for Children*, a collection of songs adapted from

3

French and German by his friends Harry Graham and Mrs. Newmarch. Adine played often at the " Proms " between 1904 and 1917, and acted for fifteen years as London critic of the *Monde Musicale*. It was at a recital she gave at St. Leonard's School, St. Andrews, in 1902, that she met Miss Frances Gray, the first High Mistress of St. Paul's Girls' School, who in the following year offered her the post of head music mistress at St. Paul's, which she gladly accepted. Of her thirty-four years' association with the school, this may not be the place to speak, but it will be permissible to quote a few lines from Miss Gray's autobiography :

It would not be easy to describe all that Mrs. O'Neill has done for the music of the School in addition to her teaching of the piano. Her pupils soon felt the influence of her strong sense of duty and of her sincerity in all she said and did. There is often a quality in a Frenchwoman's sense of duty which is like the quality of finely tempered steel. . . . Schoolgirls can have nothing more wholesome than such an example and such an influence. . . .

The school owed a further debt of gratitude to Adine, for it was she who in 1905 introduced Gustav Holst to the musical staff. After describing how she had searched in vain for some one to teach the girls singing, Miss Gray says :

I asked Mrs. O'Neill to help me and she told me of a young musician who was writing music which musicians greatly admired. He was already teaching singing in a girls' school and might be induced to come and teach us. I wrote to Gustav Holst on that day and saw him on the next.

Holst's appointment as choirmaster and musical director was much to his own benefit, as well as to that of the school, for it was in his quiet room at St. Paul's that some of his finest works, including " The Planets," were written.

The welcome Adine had given to Miss Gray's proposal was not unconnected with financial needs at home. In 1903 a son, Patrick, was born, and in 1904 Norman and Adine moved to 4 Pembroke Villas, a larger house about a quarter of a mile away, where the rest of their married life was spent. The house had a big studio built at the back, in a delightful, old-fashioned garden. To Norman, who had a great love of flowers, this garden became a joy, and he made a small lily pond for it. The neighbouring houses also had good-sized gardens, full of lilac, laburnum, and fruit trees, and—in summer especially—this was a very peaceful and countrified corner of London.

In the small things he had so far done for Martin-Harvey, Norman had already discovered that the theatre offered the inspiration and means of expressing himself for which he was searching, the opportunity of using those gifts of melody, poetical fancy, and imagination which were so abundantly his. He was therefore delighted when Martin-Harvey asked him to write the incidental music for his first production of *Hamlet* (though he fully realised the inherent difficulties of the task). The music occupied a good deal of Norman's time in 1903 and 1904, and before the production was eventually launched, his *Hamlet* overture—based on, but in stricter form than, the prelude he had composed for Martin-Harvey—had been given in Birmingham, and by Henry Wood at the Queen's Hall. On October 5, 1904, *The Times* criticised the latter performance as follows :

> Of the number of works heard in London for the first time during the present season none has attained to a higher standard than the *Hamlet* overture by Mr. Norman O'Neill, heard last night. For some years Mr. O'Neill has been slowly forging his way to the front. But, after hearing probably all of his music that has been publicly performed in London hitherto, we did not previously credit him with the power he exhibits in this, his latest, orchestral work. Of course there are signs here and there of outside influence, but there is also much that is individual and evidently characteristic of the composer himself. Mr. O'Neill's creative ideas are maturing very rapidly, and his technical equipment has always been sure and accurate ; and as the *Hamlet* overture was written only last year it may safely be said that it touches the composer's high-water mark up to the present. It contains no vain attempts at what passes for " originality," either of creative thought or of technical manipulation. It all " comes off," it is the work of a refined artist, and as such made an indubitable mark. . . .

If Norman had been susceptible to newspaper flattery his head might have been turned by this and other notices, but the following extract from a letter written to his friend George Murray, on October 19, 1904, gives an idea of the amused scepticism with which he was wont to regard the Press :

> . . . Did you hear of the last *faux pas* of the late critic of *The Standard* ? it killed him anyhow poor fellow. " Lancelot " writing of Debussy's " L'apres midi d'un Faune "—wrote FAWN. Betts, of *The Standard*, on his bed of sickness also had to write his critique, & no doubt read his pal's notice, for *he* went one better & wrote, " It is hardly to be wondered that Mr. Debussy has not managed to write anything more interesting, for his subject, the dreaming of a *young gazelle in the afternoon* is hardly a very suggestive one." It is almost too good to be true ! . . .

Norman went over to Dublin for the first performance of Martin-Harvey's *Hamlet* at the Theatre Royal on November 2. The audience gave him an ovation when he rose to conduct ; and the Dublin papers took an interest in the " rising young Irish composer," and published some rather crude portraits of him as well as several appreciative articles on his music. They congratulated him on his admirable prelude ; on not attempting to provide music for the Ghost scene ; and in general for writing music which did not distract attention from the text but " really illuminated it."

The Times also thought the music " very clever and effective " when the production came to the Lyric Theatre, London, in May 1905. Unfortunately, Londoners then had little opportunity of hearing it, for Martin-Harvey's Hamlet, coming as it did on top of revivals of the tragedy by Tree, H. B. Irving, and Frank Benson, proved ill-timed, and, after playing for a fortnight, had to be taken off. But Martin-Harvey staged three separate productions of the play (the last much influenced by Reinhardt) which proved highly successful in the provinces, Canada, and the United States over a period of twenty-five years, and Norman's music, being always performed in its entirety, gained him much notice. The production of 1904–5 was an important landmark in Norman's career : it demonstrated his unique talent and potentialities for theatrical work, and he was always grateful to Martin-Harvey for giving him the chance.

CHAPTER VI

THE MUSICAL LEAGUE

MESSRS. SCHOTT now began to look with favour on Norman's music. They had already published three piano pieces (op. 15) and two songs (op. 16), and in 1905 they published his Variations and Fugue on an Irish air for two pianos (op. 17), the theme of which, called " Moloch Mary," had been suggested to him by Mrs. Milligan Fox. Norman and Adine often played these variations at concerts, and Adine played them for the first time, with Fanny Davies, at a recital she gave in 1904. Henceforth Schott continued at regular intervals to publish Norman's piano and chamber music. In an article in *The Musical Standard* for April 1907, Joseph Holbrooke wrote :

> . . . Every real well-wisher [of contemporary English music] should at once rush to this publishing firm, and invest in all they can obtain of Mr. O'Neill's. I know they won't, but I still persevere in telling them to do these strange things ! . . . Mr. O'Neill has quite a number of his efforts at this same house, which is more than many can boast of, for it is surely a most conservative firm, for English music. . . .

In course of time Norman was able to drop some of his more irksome work, such as the Highgate school and the amateur orchestra at Penshurst. He then accepted the post of musical director and organist to the West London Ethical Society. This rather spoiled the domestic Sunday evenings, but the association with Dr Stanton Coit, the well-known preacher and leader of the ethical movement, made the work pleasant, and Norman edited the music for an *Ethical Hymn Book*.

It was in February 1906 that his overture " In Spring-time " —a counterpart to " In Autumn "—was played for the first time in Birmingham by the Halford Society. The programme made it clear that the work was not to be considered as a tone-picture of Spring itself, but rather as the impression of a parti-cular Spring on the composer's mind. On the same occasion Adine played the Mozart Concerto in C, and Norman's " Death on the Hills " was also given ;—one of the local papers said that the evening would be remembered as " the O'Neill concert." On the new overture, *The Birmingham Post* commented :

> There is in the music something of the mystery of awakening nature ; something of the rapture the renewal of vitality brings to the human parti-cipator in nature. As abstract or absolute music, the piece is good. . . .

The principal movement, besides the orthodox first and second subjects, has a wealth of thematic material, and the ideas are clothed in rich harmony, with fine orchestral colouring. Indeed, it is most striking, this mastery by our young composers of the resources of the modern orchestra. Not so many years ago English scoring used to be described as " bald " ; that is a reproach that can no longer be urged. There is rather the danger of the ambitious young writer laying on his colour with too heavy a hand, but Mr. O'Neill has struck the happy medium, and his orchestration is marked by reserve, while his climactic points are vividly realised. . . .

" In Spring-time " was well received when Henry Wood gave it at one of the " Proms " in the autumn of this year, and its reputation was enhanced by a performance under Beecham in 1908.

Other compositions on which Norman was working at about this time included the suite of six Miniatures for small orchestra, which he later arranged for full orchestra ; a fantasy for solo voices, chorus and orchestra called " Waldemar " (op. 19) ; his toccata study for piano (op. 24, 2) ; and a set of five rondels published by Cary, of which two were by W. E. Henley, one each by George Moore [1] and Arthur Symons, and the fifth was listed as " Anon." This last was a beautiful song which Frederic Austin used to sing, and which he says used to haunt him :

> The lovely isle. Where silver wavelets creep
>   Round the great rocks and crags and noble pile
> Of silent cliffs that guard in waters deep
>   The lovely isle. . . .

Norman once rather bashfully confessed to Austin that he had written the poem himself.

All this time the theatre was increasingly in his thoughts. He wrote music for his friend J. Comyns Carr's play *A Lonely Queen*, produced in New York in 1906, but his next real opportunity was afforded by an invitation from Martin-Harvey to provide music for Rosamund Langbridge's one-act play, *The Spell*. This was a weird Galway tale, full of superstition and tragedy, which was first staged in Manchester in November 1906. It played for half an hour only, but the music ran right through it and most successfully conveyed the Irish atmosphere. Well received in Manchester, the play offended Irish susceptibilities when it was presented in Dublin and there was a hostile demonstration at the end. Martin-Harvey did not lose faith in the piece, or in Norman's " mystically expressive " music. He gave it the new title of *A Tragedy of Truth*, and in June 1907 brought the production, with Henry Ainley in the leading part, to the Adelphi Theatre, London, where (as he says in his autobiography)

---

[1] George Moore told Norman that this wistful setting of " The Lilacs are in Bloom " filled him with surprise and pleasure.

" it created a profound impression." Clemens von Franckenstein
—now often in England as conductor for the Moody-Manners
opera company—conducted Norman's music, which received
particularly appreciative attention from the critics.

" Mr. O'Neill's score suffered the fate of being made an
accompaniment to conversation," thus ended the notice in *The
Morning Post*. The play brought Norman face to face with a
problem that was to worry him for the rest of his life. He realised
that only the gentle persuasion of good music played by skilled
performers could induce an audience to listen attentively to a
theatre orchestra before the opening, or in the intervals, of a
" straight " play, and he was later to achieve some success in
this direction. But to put a stop to disturbances in the course
of a play in which music played an integral part, drastic action
was needed. Martin-Harvey said in his autobiography, " The
nuisance of people arriving after a play like *A Tragedy of Truth*
has started, disturbing those who were already seated, distracting
the actors and destroying the atmosphere which Norman O'Neill's
music was creating for the full appreciation of the play, I felt
should be remedied . . ." As *A Tragedy of Truth* was given
as a curtain-raiser to *The Corsican Brothers*, he was able to make a
rule that " no late-comer was to be allowed to take his seat till
the first play was over."

That *A Tragedy of Truth* had made an impression was shown
by its selection for performance before Queen Alexandra at a
Lyceum charity matinée in July 1908, when Norman conducted.
The prelude and intermezzo were also performed at a concert
in the Pump Room, Bath. (Norman several times conducted
performances of his works there, at the invitation of the musical
director, Max Heymann, who had married Adine's friend, Edith
Meadows.)

Martin-Harvey soon found another task for him—this time
to write music for *The Bride of Lammermoor*, Stephen Phillips's
version of Scott's novel, which he intended to produce at Glasgow
in March 1908. Norman tried to put as much Scottish atmosphere
into this score as he had given Irish atmosphere to *A Tragedy of
Truth*. Particularly successful was the intermezzo between the
first and second scenes of Act III, which included an impressive
dirge for oboe and a typical Scottish reel. The production was
lavish, and it was rapturously received at Glasgow, where Norman
conducted, and elsewhere, on a provincial tour. In the cold
light of London, however, it was seen that Stephen Phillips had
failed to provide as dramatic a version of the old story as that
written by Herman Merivale and acted by Irving in the palmy

days of the Lyceum. As J. T. Grein remarked in *The Sunday Times* when the play, renamed *The Last Heir*, came to the Adelphi Theatre in the autumn : " There was something wanting in the atmosphere ; something which the poet did not grasp but which the composer . . . of the remarkably weird and forcible music expressed poignantly in his score." In the end Norman's music had a far longer life than the play, for he made out of it an effective orchestral work, called " A Scotch Rhapsody "(op. 30).

He wrote music for Martin-Harvey's production of *The World and his Wife*, in 1909. Thereafter none of Martin-Harvey's plays required his assistance, with the exception of a version of *Everyman*, called *Via Crucis*, for which he composed music when it was produced at the Garrick Theatre in 1923. But the work Norman had done for Martin-Harvey had provided valuable experience, and the reputation he had gained in the theatre was to stand him in good stead.

Norman combined with his artistic, imaginative nature, a strong vein of practicality. He was keen to see his profession organised, and was eager to help in putting the claims of music before the public. His punctual, methodical ways made him a useful colleague on committees. Thus he duly joined the Society of British Composers, which was founded by Stanley Hawley and J. B. McEwen in 1905, his name appearing among the council of the Society in 1912 ; he was an active member of the Musical Conductors' Association ; and he played a large part in the formation in 1908 of the Musical League, a concern which proved short-lived, but which had some highly distinguished sponsors.

The nucleus of the Musical League may be found in Norman's close friendship with Frederick Delius. The story of that friendship will be told in a later chapter ; here it will suffice to say that from 1907 onwards Delius was a frequent visitor at Pembroke Villas. Adine and Norman (when the Ethical Church no longer claimed him) were always " at home " to their friends on Sunday evenings, and Delius, Thomas Beecham, Balfour Gardiner, and Cyril Scott were some of those who accepted this standing invitation.

On March 23, 1908, the readers of *The Times*—or at least those who persevered to the end of one of the more obscure pages—were confronted with a letter to the editor beginning : " Sir, We ask you to give publicity to the fact that we, the undersigned, have formed a new musical society, to be known as the Musical League." Eyes no doubt travelled swiftly to the foot of the letter to see who " the undersigned " might be. They were an imposing collection, beginning with Edward Elgar (President) and Frederick Delius (Vice-President). The signatures of the members of the committee, beside Norman's, were those of Alexander C. Mackenzie, Adolph Brodsky, W. G. McNaught, Henry J. Wood, Granville Bantock, Philip L. Agnew, Percy Pitt, and Harry Evans. The treasurer was announced as Mr. J. D. Johnston of Liverpool, and the secretary as Mr. C. Copeley Harding of Birmingham. Norman himself later took over the secretaryship.

The objects of the League were thus summarised :

(a) To hold an annual festival of the utmost attainable perfection in a town where conditions are favourable. (b) To devote the programmes of these festivals to new or unfamiliar compositions, English and foreign. (c) To make use, as far as possible, of the existing musical organisations of each district, and of the services of local musicians. (d) To establish a means by which composers, executive musicians, and amateurs may exchange ideas.

The letter went on to stress the importance of encouraging local enterprise, and mentioned the good work being done in Germany by the Tonkünstler-Verein ; it stated that the subscription would be a guinea a year, and announced that Dr. Hans Richter had consented to direct the first festival of the League which, it was hoped, would be held in Manchester in the autumn.

Obviously there was much that was excellent in the aims of the League. A few—but very few—of the larger provincial towns already had separately organised musical lives of their own, and it was a worthy object to try to extend this sense of independence and healthy rivalry to other large towns. The cynics inevitably protested that members of the committee would use the League as a convenient vehicle for the performance of their own works ; as a result, a clause was inserted in the constitution debarring " any member of the committee from having a composition of his own performed at the festivals of the Musical League." Arthur Symons, giving a general welcome to the League in *The Saturday Review*, came down heavily on this clause :

. . . What hypocrisy of humility to pretend, as not only this committee, but other committees, those of painters, are pretending, that they would bring suspicion on themselves by choosing for performance a work composed by one or other of the members of them ! Here, the prospects of hearing good music are at once seriously limited, as one looks down the list of names on the committee. Why prohibit their own music, because they have to give opinion on the music of others ? The music, then, of Elgar, Delius, Mackenzie, Bantock, Pitt and O'Neill is not to be given at the festivals : where shall we find as good a list of those whose music is to be given ? . . .

The well-meaning leaguers thus found themselves, at the outset, between Scylla and Charybdis. Dr. Richter and Manchester apparently soon disappeared from their calculations. The League gave no further sign of life until November 1908, when a paragraph in *The Times* announced that a festival was to be held at Liverpool in the following spring. It was not until September 24 and 25, 1909, however, that the Liverpool Festival actually took place.

The chief reason for this delay was probably that Norman and Delius, the mainsprings of the League, were both busy men, and that Delius lived in France. Elgar, writing to Norman on June 23, 1909, to thank him for conducting two of his partsongs in Paris—the occasion will be described later,—added, " I am interested to hear of the progress of the League " ; but he does not seem to have taken an active part in its management. Norman did his utmost to make the festival a success, and sent invitations to many distinguished British and foreign musicians. Vincent d'Indy wrote from Paris to express his regret that he could not accept " l'aimable invitation que vous voulez bien me faire au nom de la Musical League."

Sir Arnold Bax, in *Farewell, my Youth*, gives a misleading impression when he says that " in September, 1909, the self-confident Musical League came to birth amid a great clamour of tuckets and tabors, and almost every English composer and outstanding executant made the pilgrimage to Liverpool for the loudly heralded event." In fact, the Musical League was already eighteen months old, and the difficulty it had found in persuading musicians to combine, and the public to take an interest in its activities, had considerably subdued any self-confidence it may once have possessed. As *The Times* said, it " trotted very quietly into its field of operations." Nevertheless, the Liverpool Festival proved a success artistically, if not financially. Three concerts were given, one for chamber music on the first day (in which the work of Balfour Gardiner, Joseph Holbrooke, Arnold Bax, and Cyril Scott was represented), and, on the next day, concerts of orchestral and choral music which included first performances of works by Vaughan Williams, Bax, Austin, and Frank Bridge. Some songs by Delius were sung, but otherwise the members of the committee abided by their undertaking not to sponsor performances of their own works. *The Times,* whose notices filled one and a half columns, declared that " the whole thing was a right effort and one well worth making " ; it applauded the use of local material for the festival, but maintained that more attention should have been given to publicity and to local conditions, for "Liverpool was scarcely aware that a festival was going on in the town, and at each concert there were rows of empty seats. . . ."

The concourse was certainly brilliant, and the committee's guests were feasted at two dinners and a lunch. Elgar was present, and spoke, while others who signed Norman's menu card were John Coates, Dr. Sanford Terry, Frederic Austin, Balfour Gardiner, Arnold Bax, and Ethel Smyth, who conducted two of her songs. Delius himself was ill and could not go to Liverpool, as he had intended. In reply to a letter from Adine, he wrote from Grez-sur-Loing on October 7, 1909 :

> Dear Mrs. O'Neill,—Many thanks for your long letter with the account of the Festival. I was so glad to hear that everything went off so well & that it was an artistic success. Two suppers and a lunch surpassed my most sanguine expectations—" I hope now that many new members will join the League." I am quite alright again altho' I have not yet started work. The weather has been muggy & wet—but yesterday and today are simply divine autumn days—sunny & still. My indisposition was a severe bilious attack— prepared in Denmark & brought to a crisis by a fortnight's stay in England— and associating with the better class of people. The English bourgeois has always this effect on me—but as I stand it, as a rule, only a day or two, it has no serious results. This time, however, I had an overdose. No other nation but the English would put up with the state of affairs you write about— " Nothing to eat after 11 p.m." *I suppose it is considered bad for you.* Please tell Norman to inform his under-secretary that Grez-sur-Loing (Seine et Marne), France, is not in England. Every communication I receive from the Musical League, I have to pay double. I must have paid about 5 francs by now. It is not the money, but I am called down every time to the postman at 8 a.m.
>
> I am also very glad that Elgar turned up and made a decent speech. With love to you both from me and Jelka.
>
> I remain yours affectionately,
>
> Frederick Delius.

The letter is typical of the sarcastic attitude adopted by Delius towards England and the English at that time, but which later he came to modify considerably. The sentence in inverted commas—" I hope now that many new members will join the League," suggests that the League was already becoming rather a joke, though for a time an attempt was still made to take it seriously.

It was hoped to hold a festival at Hanley in 1910 ; but the arrangements had to be cancelled at the last moment owing to the death of the local conductor. In 1911, the International Music Congress in London absorbed the energies of the active members of the League, and to a large extent carried out its objects. In July, 1912, *The Times* announced that a joint musical gathering of the League and the Incorporated Society of Musicians would be held in Birmingham in the following winter ; this also seems not to have materialised. *The Musical Times* made a solemn pronouncement that " The future of the League may soon have to be discussed seriously." It was so discussed ; the more Norman and his distinguished colleagues looked at it, the less future did it appear to have ; and one fine morning—no one can be quite sure of the date—the Musical League was found to have passed away, very peacefully, in its sleep.

In 1909 Schott published Norman's " Trio in F " and his " Berceuse for Violin." But the year contained events more important to his career than this, or than the Liverpool Festival of the Musical League. Before we describe them, one other episode of the year remains to be recorded—an admirable enterprise, not without its comic side, on which Norman always looked back with some amusement. This was his visit to Paris in May, 1909, as conductor of a choir of a hundred London schoolgirls, organised by the Girls' School Music Union, which took part, with five hundred French girls of the " Chorale des lycées de jeunes filles," in a " Festival Franco-Anglais " at the Trocadéro.

The proceeds of the concert were given to the " Œuvre de la protection de l'enfance contre la tuberculose." The invitation came from the French side and was eagerly accepted by Miss Cecilia Hill, who carefully selected her choir from twenty-one London secondary schools. Norman, who took Henry Wood's place as conductor, orchestrated for the occasion eight national songs of England, Scotland and Ireland : " Early one morning," " Now is the month of Maying," " O Bay of Dublin," " The Flight of the Earls," " The Rising of the Lark," " The Ash Grove," " Ye Banks and Braes," and " The Hundred Pipers." Two of Elgar's part-songs, " The Snow " and " Fly, singing bird, fly," were also included in the programme.

After half a dozen rehearsals and a preliminary concert in London, the party crossed the Channel on May 10, 1909. One of the choir was Miss Rachel Ferguson, who, in her book *Passionate Kensington,* says : " Mr. O'Neill went over with us on the boat, and I remember seeing him standing, hatless, on the deck, being secretly adored by all the schoolgirls." Perhaps this adds significance to the comment of the *Monde Musicale* on the girls at the concert, that " chacune a les yeux fixés sur le chef, M. Norman O'Neill, qui obtient un parfait ensemble."

They were received with true French hospitality. A leaflet printed for the occasion said " Carriages will stand at the disposal of the whole English party," and the carriages took them to two rehearsals at the Trocadéro, and to a reception on May 12 at the Sorbonne, where Miss Hill and Norman were made " Officiers d'Académie." The rehearsals were apparently awaited with some trepidation by the French. According to the *School Music Review* :

> Hints were allowed to drop that the souls of many good Parisians were possessed in doubt as to what manner of thing it was that they had brought into their midst in inviting this choir from a musically unenlightened isle such as Britain. Their doubts were dispelled so soon as Mr. O'Neill began to flourish his bâton. Compliments poured in. " What beauty of tone ! What unity ! How do you get them to sing together so ? " It is said that one well-known conductor remarked afterwards, " I wish we had a choir like that at the Opéra." . . .

After hearing the girls sing " The Hundred Pipers," with ever-increasing gusto and stamping of feet, Saint-Saëns said " Elles chantent comme des sauvages," which in the circumstances was probably meant as a compliment.

May 13 was devoted to an excursion to Versailles ; the festival took place on Friday, May 14. The English girls, dressed in white, were given the place of honour at the front of the platform, and, in the words of the Paris correspondent of *The Times*, they sang " with great daintiness and finish." The French girls, under Gabriel Pierné, showed a delightful sense of rhythm. Saint-Saëns conducted the Colonne orchestra in a performance of his " Phaeton," and another famous veteran, Alexandre Guilmant, played the organ ; so that, in more ways than one, this was a particularly happy occasion, which attracted a vast audience, including M. Doumergue, then Minister of Public Instruction.

On the whole, the English critics praised the French singing, and the French critics praised the English singing. " Je ne veux désobliger personne," said the critic of *La Revue Musicale*, " mais en toute sincerité, si j'avais un prix à décerner, ce n'est peut-être pas aux élèves de Paris que je l'attribuerais." *The Evening Standard* objected to the British songs chosen ; but there was general agreement that Norman had trained his forces well, and had led them gallantly in action.

CHAPTER VII

" THE BLUE BIRD "

In the early months of 1909 there occurred a development in the London theatrical world which was to have an important bearing on Norman's career. It was announced that Mr. Herbert Trench, the poet, who had retired from the Board of Education the year before, had been appointed director of the Haymarket Theatre. Trench had behind him only the limited, paid-up capital of a commercial company ; but he had determined on four salutary principles : never to put on plays which did not attain the level of repertory excellence ; to alternate the popular and the rarer kind of play ; to give a chance to young and unknown writers ; and to aim in his productions at a real union of the arts. With these objects in view, he naturally attached great importance to the choice of a musical director. It seems that Lord Howard de Walden, who was interested in the venture, first proposed Joseph Holbrooke for this post ; for some reason Holbrooke declined it, but, remembering Norman's work for Martin-Harvey, he suggested that Norman should be approached instead.

Norman eagerly accepted the offer, for, besides the opportunity of collaborating with Herbert Trench and Frederick Harrison (who was to be connected with him in the management) and writing music for good plays, it meant that he would receive a regular salary as permanent conductor—and all this in a theatre which had long been associated with a high standard of efficiency and dignified leadership. Of course these advantages were balanced by a corresponding loss to Norman's home life ; in future, Adine was left much alone in the evenings, and they could have only one short holiday together in the year.

The Haymarket had just secured the right of introducing *The Blue Bird* of Maeterlinck to English audiences. It had first been performed at the Arts Theatre, Moscow, and later (with less success) in Paris. The incidental music used hitherto had been that of an unknown Russian composer, and was of little importance. Trench rightly felt that *The Blue Bird* afforded an ideal opportunity for close partnership between text and music, and Norman, after he had read Maeterlinck's lovely play, enthusiastically agreed. But the production involved long preparation and could not be ready before the winter.

Trench decided to fill the gap with a revival of *King Lear*, and he asked Norman to write some incidental music for this play, also.

Norman was not unnaturally rather worried as to whether he could cope with all the music involved. He particularly wanted to make a success of his Haymarket debut, and thought at first of asking some other young composer to help him. For their summer holiday in 1909, Adine and Norman took rooms in a farmhouse near Steyning, Sussex, and Norman invited Gustav Holst to come down there and talk matters over. As a composer Holst was known up to that time for one or two light works full of melodic charm and clever orchestration, and Norman thought he might be the very man to collaborate with.

Holst arrived at Steyning on a very hot day, having bicycled all the way from London, hatless, under a broiling sun, and proceeded to faint from exhaustion. However, he soon recovered, and sat and partook of his meals under a shady tree. At the end of the day they persuaded him not to do any more bicycling, but to take the train back.

The idea of collaboration never came to anything, and Norman eventually decided to write the music entirely on his own. He had such a way of mapping out his day, and already so much experience, that he could produce the maximum amount of work in the minimum of time. But he had hardly a minute to spare for anything else, and in the autumn a newspaper paragraph recorded his exemption from service on the grand jury at the Old Bailey. "The Clerk : But you were excused at the previous sessions ? Mr. O'Neill : Yes, upon the same grounds."

King Lear was performed on September 8, 1909. Herbert Trench's rare understanding of Shakespeare made it a beautiful, indeed a memorable, production. Norman McKinnel's performance as Lear was unequal, but, at its best, very fine, and the play was graced by some exquisite scenes designed by Charles Ricketts. The music blended subtly with the scenery, and old folk songs and melodies were effectively used to create a primitive Celtic atmosphere.

Francis Toye, writing in *Vanity Fair*, said that, though he disliked all incidental music to Shakespeare, it was a pleasure " to see a modernist like Mr. O'Neill among the terribly orthodox ranks of theatre composers." He acknowledged with gratitude that Norman " once and once only provided music to be spoken through," and he was particularly pleased with the soft and intimate music after Act I, built up on a " Cordelia-motif."

Norman conducted the Queen's Hall orchestra in a performance of the music at Earl's Court in 1912, when the programme consisted entirely of works inspired by *King Lear*, including Weingartner's symphonic poem and Berlioz's overture.

After a short run of *King Lear*, all energies at the Haymarket were devoted to *The Blue Bird*. Though the stage directions made it almost indispensable in several places, Maeterlinck did not favour the idea of much incidental music for his play. Like some other poets and mystics, he has never shown much interest in music, and perhaps has not fully appreciated all the help it can give to the imagination. Debussy found this attitude rather disappointing when he met Maeterlinck and played to him his music for *Pelléas et Mélisande*. However, in the case of *The Blue Bird*, Maeterlinck left it to the Haymarket management to decide who should write the music, and how much should be written. Norman took his opportunity, and, after a careful study of the text, he composed music which, while never obtrusive, was woven into the structure of the play and helped more than one situation to a successful climax. It was necessarily elaborate, because the lighting effects and the music went hand in hand. So completely did Norman show his understanding of the poetry of the play that one critic went so far as to declare that he had done for Maeterlinck what Grieg had done for Ibsen.

When Maeterlinck, very shy and reserved, came to London for the dress rehearsal, he did say he thought there was too much music, though he agreed that it was charming. But the enthusiasm shown at the first night, on December 8, 1909, swept away all objections. The production proved a triumph for everyone—from the brilliant producer, Lyall Swete, and the scene painters and designers, Cayley Robinson, S. H. Sime and Joseph Harker, to young Olive Walter and Pauline Gilmer, who played Tyltyl and Mytyl, and the rest of the clever cast, which included Ernest Hendrie as the Dog, Norman Page as the Cat, Ina Pelly as Water, Doris Lytton as Milk, and H. R. Hignett as Sugar. A friend of William Elkin, the music publisher, was in the theatre, and telephoned to Norman afterwards to suggest that he should show the music to Elkin. Norman did so immediately, and his name was soon added to the long list of modern composers whose work Elkin published—among them Elgar, Scott, Quilter and Bantock.

The Blue Bird established Norman in the public mind as a composer of great charm and delicacy, and from this time until his death he ranked as *facile princeps* among composers for the

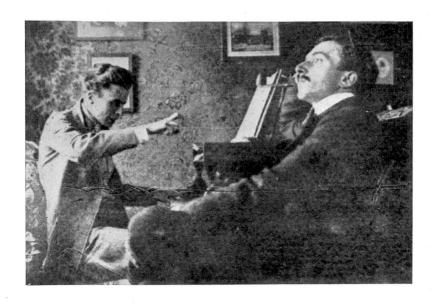

V.—IN NORMAN O'NEILL'S LODGINGS AT FRANKFORT

(*Above*) Norman with a dramatic forefinger plays to Clemens von Franckenstein, who is duly impressed.

VI.—(*Below*) Franckenstein gives a soulful recital to Norman, who is equally touched.

VII.—ADINE O'NEILL AT THE TIME OF HER MARRIAGE

theatre. The four dances from the play—" The Dance of the Mist Maids," " The Dance of Fire and Water," " The Dance of the Stars," and " The Dance of the Hours "—were played no less than three times at the Promenade Concerts in the autumn of 1910, and the suite soon established itself as a minor classic for orchestra. The first production of *The Blue Bird* ran until June 1910 ; it was revived at the Haymarket the following Christmas, and at the Queen's Theatre at Christmas 1911. For a new act called " The Palace of Happiness," written by Maeterlinck for these revivals, Norman composed the delightful " Dance of the Joys " ; which was also published by Elkin.

One of the most impressive moments in *The Blue Bird* is when the unborn children sail in Time's galley down to earth, and there is heard " as though issuing from the depths of the abyss " a " distant song of gladness and expectation." " What is that ? " asks Tyltyl. " It is not they singing. . . . It sounds like other voices . . ." and Light replies : " Yes, it is the song of the mothers coming out to meet them." The song as Norman composed it was a chorus without words, but Mrs. William Elkin provided some words for it on its publication. In his book of reminiscences, Mr. W. H. Leverton, for many years box-office manager at the Haymarket, tells the following story :

. . . At matinées, teas are served in the auditorium of the Haymarket, and in order that the tea shall be made at the right moment, a girl keeps an eye on the action of the play, and tells the girl who makes the tea when it is time to do so.

When *The Blue Bird* was being played, there was a beautiful piece of music by Norman O'Neill, known as " The Song of the Mothers," and it was amusing to see, as I often did, a girl rush up to the tea-counter and cry : " Time to make, Ashie " (Miss Ash was the young lady who made the tea), " —Song of the Mothers." . . .

Besides publishing a piano selection from Norman's music, and the dances and " The Song of the Mothers " separately, Elkin published for orchestra and piano a " Blue Bird Waltz," composed by Norman from melodies in the play. He also brought a successful action in the Chancery Courts to restrain Messrs. Francis, Day and Hunter " from the publication of a waltz which had been put upon the market, and which plaintiffs said deceived purchasers into the belief that they were buying music from the well-known play, *The Blue Bird*." There was no suggestion of plagiarism, only of what is legally termed " passing off."

The waltz to which exception was taken was composed by Mr. Charles Coote and published, with a large blue bird on the

4

cover, on February 4, 1910, about a fortnight after Elkin had published Norman's dances. Norman was joined as a co-plaintiff, and his evidence on certain musical technicalities inspired some typically judicial jokes from Mr. Justice Eve. It was an important case which lasted for several days, and has been cited in legal text-books. Francis Toye and Herbert Trench both testified to the importance of the music in the play, and Herbert Trench said that it was " essential " to the great success of *The Blue Bird*. Evidence was given that Mr. Coote's waltz had actually been bought by some one under the impression that he was obtaining Norman's music.

Mr. Coote maintained that he had composed his waltz two years earlier and had suggested the title " L'Oiseau Bleu " in August 1909, before he had heard of Maeterlinck's play; but Mr. Justice Eve held that, consciously or subconsciously, he must have been influenced by the advance publicity for the Haymarket production. On the question which had been raised of the status of the music, the Judge considered that " the music plays an important part in the play, that it is excellent music, that it is appropriate, and that it is of importance in this production." Judgment was given for the plaintiffs.

Punch indulged in this parody of the proceedings :

Counsel. My lord, I appear for the plaintiffs, who contend that the defendant firm has infringed their copyright.

The Judge. A case of copy-wrong (*laughter*).

Counsel. So I hope to show, if your lordship will permit me. To continue, the plaintiff firm acquired, in 1908, the sole right in the music for a play entitled *The Red Lobster*. This, as you probably are aware, was a great success.

The Judge. It always gives me indigestion (*laughter*).

Counsel. Among the musical numbers was a waltz air.

The Judge. Ah, you should take this case to the Appeal Court. That's where they reverse (*laughter*).

Counsel. A few weeks after the plaintiffs had issued this, under the title " The Red Lobster Waltz," the defendants published a waltz, under the title " L'Homard Rouge "—

The Judge. Is there an interpreter in court ? (*laughter*)—

Counsel. Which, I need hardly inform your lordship, means the same thing.

The Judge. Yes, but in French. They took French leave, in fact (*laughter*).

Counsel. And not only was the title the same, but the music also. If your lordship will examine the copies of the two waltzes which I have here, you will see . . .

The Judge. Help ! (*Laughter.*) What are these little dots ?

Counsel. Those are notes, my lord.

The Judge. They're not like my notes (*laughter*). And what are these lines ?

Counsel. Those are bars, my lord.

The Judge. Ah ! (*laughter*). And what is this mark ?

Counsel. That is a rest, my lord.

The Judge. A rest in a bar (*laughter*). A very pleasant thing, too (*more laughter*). By no means confined to musicians (*loud laughter*).

[And so on.]

The production of *The Blue Bird* threw down a challenge to managers and public alike on the whole question of their attitude towards theatre music. Audiences had chattered persistently during the *entr'actes* of *King Lear*, and in *The Blue Bird* they were almost as bad. The unusual excellence of Norman's music raised the question in an unusually acute form. *The Times* recognised this in an admirable article on January 8, 1910 :

. . . No one to whom music means anything can have seen *The Blue Bird* without lamenting that Mr. Norman O'Neill's charming overture and *entr'actes* should have to fight for a hearing against the talking of a whole audience. The audience is not entirely to blame. Theatre music is not meant, as a rule, to be listened to ; and audiences have grown into a habit which, if they knew it, detracts enormously from their enjoyment in the rare cases where music has been worthily used. For the talking between the acts of *The Blue Bird* rouses a suspicion that the audience is not really listening to the music played while the curtain is up, and is missing things as beautiful to the ear as the appearance of Time's ship is to the eye or the lilies in the tombstones to the mind, and, still worse, is missing an essential part of the production. There is no question but that Mr. O'Neill knew *The Blue Bird* pretty thoroughly before he set to work on his score, that he had caught the atmosphere of the play, and absorbed its artistic impression. How much the production has gained by the beauty of his appeal to the ear could only be learned from seeing a performance from which was omitted all the music that can possibly be described as incidental. For his object has evidently been not merely to provide a musical accompaniment to the play, but to make something which should have its structure, just as much as the play has its structure, the two agreeing with each other, supporting and elucidating each other throughout. That is the obvious way of writing theatre music ; and, as usual with the obvious way, is the right way. . . . Perhaps if *The Blue Bird* were advertised as a ' musical play ' the audiences at the Haymarket would surrender themselves more readily to the influence that is waiting to prolong and intensify the mood, instead of snapping it short with violent contrast or blundering ineptitude.

But it needs a change in our whole attitude towards theatre music, whether played when the curtain is down or when it is up, to give managers and public a proper return for their money. . . . The scope of music in the drama might be greatly enlarged, and every play into which music enters at all should be looked upon as a play which depends for part of its effect upon that music. . . . Before we can reform our theatre music we need to realise first that music is a legitimate and may be a necessary part of the art of drama, and next that every play worth its salt has a character which music can help us to feel and to understand. Not only music but the drama suffers from the present divorce or hopelessly patched-up union.

It is a pity that the professed musical plays of our own time offer so little encouragement. Opera lies outside the present discussion. . . . Of musical comedy nothing can be hoped. . . .

There is another point of view from which the advancement of the place of music in the drama is perhaps worth consideration. A good deal is heard to-day of the lack of opportunity for English composers. Here is a field in which there is ample room for good work. . . . When music receives as much consideration in the theatre as the scenery there will be a brisk demand for new music specially composed for new productions. Such music may not live for ever ; but it would at least live for the run of the play ; and would so stand a chance of more performances than are enjoyed by the ordinary concert-room suite or overture. And the time would come when audiences would pay the same attention to the music as they do to the scenery. . . .

There was a time when it seemed that the hopes expressed in this article might be nearing fulfilment, but by the end of the 1920's they were further from realisation than they were in 1910. The hope of a revival in public appreciation of good theatre music has since become more remote than ever ; yet in a changing world there is always room for optimism.

As soon as Norman began work at the Haymarket, he felt that it would be a great aid to atmosphere if the orchestra pit could be covered over, so that the audience could hear the music without having any of their attention distracted from the stage. During the run of *The Blue Bird* he succeeded only in having it partially covered,—and in order to be able to dim the lighting as much as possible, he hit on the ingenious idea of having the orchestral parts scored with white notes on black. Later, palm leaves entirely obscured the orchestra and its conductor. (" You are *so* beautiful," cried Mrs. Patrick Campbell, " and they hide you under the palm trees ! ")

For the production of *The Blue Bird* Norman was fortunate in having as his assistant at the Haymarket such an excellent musician as Geoffrey Toye. There were several provincial tours of the play during the years 1909–12, for some of which Norman conducted (he did so at Dublin in October 1911), while Toye took charge of the others. Miss Margaret Drew has set down the following memories :

I would like to say how the dancers—of whom I was one—in the late Herbert Trench's production of *The Blue Bird* in 1909–12, all loved Mr. Norman O'Neill who was then conducting his own exquisite music for that unforgettably beautiful play. Mr. O'Neill used to spoil us with large boxes of chocolates and other luxuries, and was the very kindest of friends to us. When, during one of the *Blue Bird* tours, I—at a moment's notice—had to "go on" for my principal (who had hurt her foot) in the rôle of Water, it was he who encouraged me, calming my nervousness, and afterwards writing me a delightful note praising my performance (much more, I am sure, than it merited !). When he died I felt I had lost a real friend—though I cannot claim to have known him well—for his thoughtfulness, charm and enchanting humour endeared him, I know, to all the *Blue Bird* company.

Why Maeterlinck's play has not been revived more often in later years is something of a mystery. There was an extremely successful tour in Australia in 1912, with Claude Rains as stage manager ; and there have since been one or two less successful English revivals with reduced music and scenery ; but it is surprising that *The Blue Bird* has not been given regularly at Christmas, for it is a play for young and old, with such beauty and depth of thought that it should survive the years and fashions.

When Norman was asked why the play was not revived on a proper scale, he said he thought it was because the production was expensive and required a large company and a fairly large orchestra ; but he maintained that it could have been simplified for the purpose without losing its attractiveness. The B.B.C., too, might take a hint from the Australian broadcasting authorities, who sponsored an excellent performance of play and music at Christmas 1937, for *The Blue Bird* lends itself particularly to radio.

CHAPTER VIII

FROM DUNSANY TO IBSEN

NORMAN O'NEILL's talent as a composer lay not only in his rich store of tunes and melodies, but also in knowing how to orchestrate music for a very limited number of players. At this difficult art he became a past master. However small the means at his disposal, he always managed to make his theatre music sound polyphonic and rich, making good use of string and wind instruments and employing brass with great discretion. His poetical, imaginative mind fitted him to understand the theatre, and it came easily to him to adapt his musical thoughts to the moods and circumstances of different plays. His sense of method served him well in planning and timing his music, and experience taught him how to lengthen or shorten a musical phrase without impairing its proportion or shape—a feat often made necessary by last-minute changes at rehearsals. He left nothing to chance, and went into the smallest details with producers and stage-managers ; his music was first sketched down on a single line, then written for piano (as a piano was used at rehearsals), and finally orchestrated.

At work and with his musicians, Norman was a disciplinarian, always punctual himself and expecting other people to be so. There was no Bohemian *laissez-aller* in his manner of life or in his dealings with others, and this made him an excellent colleague. Enjoying the incentive of working for a definite purpose, he never found it irksome to compose " on demand " ; but it was natural that the better the play on which he was engaged, the better would be the music it inspired. He was fortunate in having rarely to deal with inferior plays ; and it was only towards the end of his life (when he had to write for absurdly small theatre orchestras and could not obtain the effects he wanted) that he was ever unhappy about his work.

In an article in a musical paper Norman once wrote : " Melodies occur to me in all sorts of circumstances—on the top of a bus, during a meal, in the course of a walk, at a play—anywhere, in fact. Sometimes I jot them down on the spot, and keep them for use when a suitable opportunity arises, but often enough I just make a mental note of them." When a tune or melody was needed, he did not always rely on the inspiration of the moment, but would often tap his store of memories. In the midst of composing he would walk out of his studio, do some gardening and return refreshed to his work, probably having overcome some difficulty, or with a tune in his mind ready to be written down.

During the year or so that followed the production of *The Blue Bird* several plays were given at the Haymarket which made only slight demands on Norman's talent, among them *Don* by Rudolf Besier ; *Priscilla Runs Away* by Countess Arnim (for this he wrote a waltz published by Chappell) ; and Charles McEvoy's *All that Matters*, which required some preludes. Norman was thus able to devote himself to building up and training his orchestra, which gradually obtained a considerable reputation. Among his principals were several well-known players who for the sake of a regular salary were glad to play at a theatre where only good music was performed, under a musician whom they respected. They were attracted, too, by the covering of palm leaves which so distressed Mrs. Patrick Campbell, for it enabled them to preserve a desired incognito.

The anxious care taken by Norman to ensure that music at the Haymarket should be the best possible, is shown by the following paragraphs from *The Times* of March 8, 1911 :

The question of what music should be played in the theatre, or indeed whether there should be any at all, is open to any amount of discussion, but one good practical example is worth a great deal of discussion, and there is one such example at the present time in the musical programme which Mr. Norman O'Neill provides at the Haymarket between the acts of *All that Matters*.

The first movement of Mozart's "Jupiter" Symphony is played, and very well played too, a quarter of an hour before the curtain rises, for the benefit of the pit and the gallery and the few people in the better parts of the house who are fortunate enough to come early. Mr. O'Neill has written some characteristic music to introduce each act, music which has strong and attractive melody and which is pleasantly scored. In the intervals he has arranged a number of things which seem to have the right qualities for the purpose, since they are not so serious as to depress those of the audience who are not musical, while they are full of interest to those who care to listen. Two charming little pieces by Fiocco, one of the family of 18th century musicians who came from Venice and settled in Brussels, have been very gracefully scored for the modern orchestra and are delightful to hear in the first interval. In the later ones there are a delicate Minuet by Mozart, an exceedingly taking little piece by Mr. Waldo Warner, called "Fairy's Dance," and, lastly, a very beautiful Danish melody which Mr. Percy Grainger has arranged. Lest anyone should object that they are not given tunes which they know, the Barcarolle from *Tales of Hoffmann* is also included in the scheme, and since it is played with the same refinement and care which is given to the other pieces it does not sound incongruous even after Mozart.

That was a remarkable programme for a theatre orchestra, and it remains a testimony to Norman's energy and enthusiasm. For several weeks of 1914 he even played a different programme of music at each performance in the week. Proof of the seriousness with which he studied his work at the Haymarket may be found in his excellent paper on " Music to Stage Plays," printed at the end of this book, which was given to the Musical Association in 1911 and aroused much interest in the Press at the time. The reader may be referred to it for fuller details of Norman's technique in composing and conducting for the stage.

In the meantime more of Norman's music was being heard in the concert-room. His setting for baritone and orchestra of Keats's ballad " La Belle Dame sans Merci " (op. 31) was sung for the first time by Frederic Austin at the Queen's Hall in January 1910. Norman conducted the New Symphony Orchestra in this performance of what Francis Toye, in *Vanity Fair*, called " an altogether delightful piece of work, full of imagination, poetry and sensitive response to the varying atmosphere of the poem." The ballad made a further deep impression when it was given at two matinées at the Haymarket in June 1912, in aid of the fund for preserving the house in Rome in which Keats died. Frederic Austin again sang as the Knight, while Frederick Ranalow took the part of the Woodman, into whose mouth Norman put the first three interrogatory stanzas. (Later, Norman revised and re-orchestrated this work, the first performance of the new version being sung by George Baker for the B.B.C. at Savoy Hill in 1927).

In January 1910, Adine played in public in Paris for the last time. At the Salle Erard she played Norman's " Trio in F " (op. 32) with D. Lederer and H. Choinet, and the Variations and Fugue on an Irish Air for two pianos (op. 17) with Motte Lacroix. These variations were now fairly well known, but to give them a wider opportunity of being heard, Norman had scored them for orchestra ; and the orchestral version was first performed at a Promenade Concert under Henry Wood on September 14, 1911. " The orchestration," said *The Times* the next morning, " though a little heavy in some of the early variations, is generally picturesque and adds considerably to the effect of the valse, the slow movement in D minor, and the entry of the theme *fortissimo* and *maestoso* near the end. The middle section is the most beautiful, for the valse gives relief just at the right moment between the lovely *Andante* and the plaintive *Adagio*, and the *Coda* . . . makes a simple and beautiful finish to the whole."

The next production at the Haymarket which called for serious attention from Norman was Lord Dunsany's one-act play, *The Gods of the Mountain*, staged in June 1911 as a curtain-raiser to Rudolf Besier's comedy *Lady Patricia*. *The Gods of the Mountain* is an oriental fantasy about seven beggars of the city of Kongros, who pretend to be the seven gods whose images in jade are famous in their mountain shrine a day and a half's journey away. Led by a master beggar (magnificently played at the Haymarket by C. V. France) the beggars overcome the doubts of the inhabitants, and are about to be entertained with wine, women and song, when the real gods enter, prancing slowly, and turn them into stone. This finally convinces the citizens of the divinity of the beggars, and they prostrate themselves before the seven, crying, " We doubted them ; they have turned to stone because we doubted them."

The fantasy was well calculated to inspire Norman to a happy musical collaboration, and he wrote music that was almost uncannily appropriate and fitted the text like hand and glove. Two dances from the play were published for piano by Schott. Not long afterwards Herbert Trench announced his retirement from the directorship of the Haymarket, where he left *Bunty Pulls the Strings* in the full tide of success; and in November 1912 Frederick Harrison put on another one-act play by Lord Dunsany called *The Golden Doom*, not perhaps such an effective play as *The Gods of the Mountain*, but affording even better opportunities for a composer.

The Golden Doom is an allegory about a prosperous king who ruled in the mythical city of Zericon " some while before the fall of Babylon." It tells how a boy and girl come to the iron door of the king's palace, because the boy wants to pray for a little hoop. The girl is rather proud of having made up a poem, and she recites it :

> I saw a purple bird
> Go up against the sky,
> And it went up and up
> And round about did fly.

To which the boy adds : " I saw it die."

Then, to show how clever he is, the boy writes the verse with a piece of gold on the king's door ; and the pair run away. When the mysterious writing is discovered, the king and his court and his priests are filled with terror, for they assume the stars have pronounced the doom of His Majesty. The only thing which might propitiate them, they think, is for the king that night to make a sacrifice of his " cast-off pride," by putting

his sceptre and his crown—a golden circlet—outside the door.
He does so ; and when the children come back in the early
morning they find waiting for them the answer to their prayers—
a little hoop and a stick to hit it with ! The boy runs off happily,
driving the " hoop " before him, and the king and his court, when
they wake up, are equally pleased to find that the sacrifice has
been accepted and that " the stars are satisfied."

This poetical but at the same time biting little allegory
inspired Norman to write some of his most beautiful incidental
music. Without attempting to conjure up sounds that might
have dated from before the fall of Babylon, he gave his score a
quaint oriental tone that harmonised with the scenery of S. H.
Sime and Joseph Harker, and with the whole eastern picture
described by one critic : " the iron gates of the carved palace,
the great pillars and the palm-trees, the King's curled beard,
the shaven priests of the stars, the strange naked spies that wind
and dart about the King's coming and going, the huge soldiers
who shade their faces when they look at him." Frederick Corder,
who taught so many famous composers at the R.A.M., wrote
to Norman that he was :

> Quite delighted with your music to *The Golden Doom*. I am somewhat
> of a specialist in the matter of dramatic music and must make you my un-
> reserved congratulations on yours, which was just what it ought to be. . . .
> You have wielded your slender forces with the hand of knowledge and ex-
> perience and could not have done better. I hope you may get many more
> such chances, for they are delightful to the soul of the musician.

There are many, including Francis Toye, who believe that
Norman's scores for *The Gods of the Mountain* and *The Golden Doom*
represent his finest achievements in the theatre. They gave much
pleasure to Lord Dunsany, who more than twenty years afterwards wrote that he remembered the music very vividly.

We have seen that Norman used to play at the Haymarket
his arrangements of pieces by the early eighteenth-century
composer J. H. Fiocco. In August 1912, three dances by Fiocco,
which he had arranged and orchestrated, were heard at a
Promenade Concert. Norman preserved the character of the
dances while giving them a colour that accentuated their vitality,
and, as *The Times* said, they were " quite worth the trouble."
Over a long period of years Norman made many arrangements
from Fiocco, usually for piano and violin, ten of which were
published by Schott.

In 1912 and 1913—it was in these years that the Musical
League finally passed out of existence—Balfour Gardiner's

enterprise and generosity forwarded the cause of contemporary music by giving London two series of delightful choral and orchestral concerts. At one of Balfour Gardiner's concerts, in May 1912, Norman conducted and Frederic Austin sang " La Belle Dame sans Merci " ; at another, in February 1913, Norman conducted his " Introduction, Mazurka, and Finale " (op. 43). The latter work, which had been given its first performance at a Philharmonic Society's concert in the preceding month, consisted of dances from Norman's music to *A Forest Idyll* by Charles Maude, a one-act ballet in which the chief figures were Pan with his pipes, a princess and a faun. The music was so well suited to its original purpose that (as is often the case with good ballet music) it seemed in the Queen's Hall rather to lack its associate ; but it was appreciated for its grace and melody, as well as for its unpretentiousness.

Balfour Gardiner did not continue his concerts after 1913. He had some trouble with the orchestra players, who, according to Sir Arnold Bax, were " tough." In fact, Gardiner told Bax that the last concert of the 1913 series, which included Bax's " In the Faery Hills," would have to be cancelled ; and in his autobiography Bax suggests that it was Norman's influence as an intermediary that induced him to change his mind.

The first production in England of Ibsen's chronicle play *The Pretenders* (in William Archer's translation) at the Haymarket in February 1913, gave Norman a more serious theme, and one far removed from fantasy or pastoral ballet. *The Pretenders* was not a play that particularly appealed to him, for he lacked instinctive sympathy with the rugged warriors of thirteenth-century Norway ; but he realised the opportunity it presented for music that would set and sustain the heroic note. Just as he had avoided writing conventional oriental music for Lord Dunsany's plays, so in *The Pretenders* he did not vainly seek the Norwegian harmonic idiom. A fairly liberal yet judicious use of brass helped his music, always dignified, to fit the epic quality of the saga. There was an expressive overture, and the long play with its five acts and several scenes called for a number of interludes, choruses and songs—one of which, " King Håkon's Lullaby," published by Elkin, was often sung at concerts. Certain devotional choruses were needed, and Norman had the chance to show his skill in writing for, training, and conducting a select choir of male and female voices.

For the acting of Laurence Irving, the scenery of Sime and Harker, Lyall Swete's genius as producer, as well as for the recognition, however tardy, which it afforded to one of Ibsen's masterpieces, this production of *The Pretenders* has its place in theatrical history. But the attitude of the audience towards the music, even at the Haymarket, still left much to be desired. The critic of the *Musical Standard*, writing of Norman's " eminently satisfactory " contribution, said : " If proof were needed that a London theatre audience is mostly devoid of discrimination, manners, and æsthetic taste, the final orchestral and choral music, which is of a devotional character and which accompanies a scene in the courtyard of the convent, was performed to vociferous applause of the actors, two of whom were busily enacting the part of a corpse." The music to *The Pretenders* was heard again in a broadcast performance in November 1928.

The Pretenders was taken off after three months, to be followed at the Haymarket by *Within the Law*, which ran for nearly a year but required no special music. During the remainder of 1913 Norman was at work on his " Blossom Songs," translated from the Japanese and eventually orchestrated for Roland Hayes ; and on his overture " Humoresque " (op. 47) for full orchestra, light and fantastic in character, with constantly changing moods, which was first performed at the conference of the Incorporated Society of Musicians in London in January 1914.

It was in the years immediately preceding the war of 1914–18 that he began to suffer from a disability which was to become increasingly painful and troublesome, and which sometimes demanded all his cheerfulness and courage. Massage treatment after a sharp attack of sciatica, caused by sleeping in a damp bed at a French country inn, left him with varicose veins in the legs. In the summer of 1913, when he went with his friend Charles La Trobe, the stage manager at the Haymarket, for a holiday in Germany, he had the misfortune to graze the bone of his worst leg while climbing some steep steps into a railway carriage. This brought on an ulcer, which troubled him for several years, until he benefited in 1917 from treatment at Matlock.

Later in that summer of 1913, Norman went with Adine to hear *Parsifal* at Bayreuth, and then to see Rothenburg and to stay with Clemens von Franckenstein for the Mozart festival in Munich. Varicose veins made war service out of the question for Norman, and his and Adine's work was actually little affected by the war ; the theatres did well, and London life was not much disturbed. Norman wrote music for special matinées of Thomas W. Broadhurst's play *The Holy City* in May 1914, but, as it happened, the plays put on at the Haymarket between 1914 and 1918 made few demands on him. He wrote a prelude and interludes for Jerome K. Jerome's *The Great Gamble* ; *Quinneys* and *The Mayor of Troy*, successes of 1915 and 1916, did not call for much assistance.

The concerts of the Royal Philharmonic Society were kept up throughout the war. Norman had been elected an associate of the Society in 1912, and a member and honorary director in 1913, his experience making him invaluable as a selector of orchestral players ; he was soon to undertake further responsibilities in connection with the Society. Among his activities of the early war years, mention must be made of his original music for Valerie Wingate's dramatised scenes from Longfellow's " Hiawatha "—a useful publication for schools and amateur societies brought out in 1916 ; of his music for Miles Malleson's little play, *Paddly Pools* ; [1] and of his " Hornpipe " (op. 48), composed during the winter of 1915–16. The " Hornpipe " has become one of Norman's most popular orchestral works ; first performed at Harrogate, it was given at a Promenade Concert under Henry Wood in September 1916, and eventually published for full and small orchestra.

In January 1916, Adine and Norman rejoiced greatly at the birth of their second child, a daughter. Frederick Delius took a keen interest in the baby and himself suggested that he should be her godfather ; and Mrs. Delius and Dorothy East (a former pupil of Adine) were the godmothers. She was given the names Yvonne Patricia.

[1] I wish your music could sound through this little book as it does through my head ! wrote the author to Norman in July 1916, when *Paddly Pools* was published.

CHAPTER IX

O'NEILL AND DELIUS

In an earlier chapter we saw something of the part played by Delius and Norman in the brief career of the Musical League. It is now time to say more about Norman's association with the musical genius who became his daughter's godfather. Delius had many friends among musicians, but he had a particular affection for Norman, a feeling which anyone who knew Norman will readily understand. Norman was equally fond of Delius, and the tie between the two families was drawn still closer by the friendship between Delius's wife Jelka and Adine.

Delius first visited Pembroke Villas in 1907, when he came to London to hear the first performance in England of his "Appalachia," given by the New Symphony Orchestra conducted by Fritz Cassirer. For this occasion Norman wrote the programme note describing the work. Delius came to supper ; they were a gay party, and Delius amused them by being highly satirical about the English and their ways. He altered many of his views when he got to understand England better, but at this time he was always criticising details, such as the licensing laws, or would say, " Look at the way they make their beds, the mattresses are never re-made regularly. You never see any bedding airing in open windows as you do in France ! "

The music of Delius became known in London only gradually during Edwardian days ; but from the beginning Norman and Adine were among Delius's warmest admirers and supporters. Norman's sympathies in poetry and music, of course, lay entirely with the romantics. Like most musicians of his generation, his first deep musical emotions had been stirred by Wagner (he had a treasured memory of the first time he heard, in Frankfort, the prelude to *Tristan and Isolde*). Another real revelation to him had been the modern Russian music of Moussorgsky, Tschaikovsky, Balakirev, and others, introduced to London by Henry Wood in the 'nineties. Bizet's *Carmen* he considered the perfect example of what an opera should be ; and in fact he was always charmed by the clear, concise quality of French music and orchestration. When Debussy's score of " L'Après-midi d'un Faune " came out, he marvelled at " so much being expressed with such sobriety of means, not one note too many, nor too few." But in later life he was more moved by Delius's music than by any other. From the first, he understood its poetical beauty and Delius's conception of the spiritual side of Nature.

Whether Delius's music was inspired by the stern mountains of Norway, by the smiling charm of a French river, by the throbbing pulse of a great city (Paris), or by a poem such as " Sea-drift," it did not matter, the underlying emotion, serenity and beauty of sound were to Norman an unfailing source of delight. He often said that he owed to Delius some of his deepest emotions in music, and he referred to the end of " Sea-drift " as one of the most poignant things he had ever heard—indeed, he was generally speechless for some time after it.

From 1907 onwards, Thomas Beecham was Delius's staunch and devoted champion. Henry Wood had already given performances of some of Delius's works ; but Beecham deserves the credit for establishing Delius's reputation in England. Delius often told Norman that no other conductor understood his works so well, or could give such subtle and sensitive interpretations of them. Norman, for his part, felt that Beecham was one of the great assets of English musical life ; he had the greatest admiration for his conducting, and for that forceful temperament of his which can instil life and keenness into an orchestra.

Beecham often came to Pembroke Villas, with Balfour Gardiner and other mutual friends, when Delius was staying with the O'Neills. His wit and his unorthodox ways were always a source of mirth. Norman was actually the witness of an incident which has become legendary. Beecham, wearing a thick overcoat, once met Norman in Piccadilly and started to walk with him, and talk. It was a very hot spring day. Taking off his coat, Beecham hailed a taxi, threw the coat inside, shut the door, told the driver " Follow us ! "—and went on walking.

Norman and Adine went to stay with the Deliuses at Grez-sur-Loing in 1908, the first of many visits ; and Delius and his wife stayed at Pembroke Villas when they came to London in December 1909 for the first performance of A Mass of Life (conducted by Beecham) and In a Summer Garden. Delius was always rather helpless with the orchestra at rehearsals, and Adine remembers him sitting in the stalls at the Queen's Hall listening to a rehearsal of A Mass of Life, and during some obscure passages yelling loudly, in an anguished voice, " There is something wrong somewhere ! " but being quite unable to say what was wrong, or even where. The first performance of In a Summer Garden, at a Philharmonic concert, was one of the rare occasions on which Delius conducted in person. He

was very nervous and conducted rather tamely (in fact he had
no gift for it), but the next day he came to Adine holding
the cheque he had received for conducting and beaming with
a childish delight at having earned, for the first time in his
life, some money for taking part in an actual performance.   He
asked her to take him to her Kensington bank, for he was anxious
to have the cheque turned into cash as soon as possible.

A letter from Jelka Delius, written to Adine in March 1911,
reads like a warning of the dreadful illness with which Delius
was to be afflicted ten years later :

. . . Fred is very much better, but still he needs constant care and
looking after, and I am by nature so anxious for him. . . . The cure in
Dresden only made Fred worse—awfully thin and haggard—and he only
picked up in Wiesbaden, and everybody thinks he looks very well now.   He
is working again and we take nice walks.   He had quite overrated his nerves
. . . and I was quite glad that Beecham did not do an opera of his this winter
and that he could rest. . . . He is now correcting the proofs of the Dowson
cycle, edited by Leuckart and called 'Songs of Sunset.'   I translated the
poems into German, which was fearfully difficult. . . .

"Songs of Sunset" were given their first performance by
Beecham at the Queen's Hall in June of that year.

Delius often relieved the solitude at Grez by making journeys
to all parts of Europe, but he was always glad to return home.
In the summer of 1914 he again stayed with the O'Neills ; and
he wrote to Adine from Grez on July 16 :

MY DEAR ADINE,—Just a word to thank you for the pleasant few days I
spent with you & Norman & also to tell you how comfortable & at home
I felt.

I am sorry I saw so little of you both after my departure for Hobart
Place.   The rest of my time in London was a sort of fever & passed away
like a flash—Russian ballet, dinners, suppers at 2 a.m. & luncheons.   Thank
goodness I am now back again in Grez & enjoying the quiet & our lovely
garden.

With love to you both from me & Jelka,—I remain ever yours,
                                                FREDERICK DELIUS.

The quiet was rudely shattered by the outbreak of war on
August 4, and the following letter from Delius to Norman shows
what he and Jelka had to go through in the ensuing weeks :

" GREZ-SUR-LOING, SEINE ET MARNE,
                    15th Sept. 1914.

MY DEAR NORMAN,—I received yesterday your letter & 2 papers dated
14th and 15th August.   I had received once before another envoi—many
thanks !   We have been seeing life since I wrote you last.   From towards
the end of August up to the 7th of September there was an ever-growing
panic here.   The high road to Fontainebleau was a terrifying sight.   As you

VIII.—NORMAN CONDUCTING THE CHOIR OF LONDON SCHOOLGIRLS AT THE TROCADÉRO, PARIS,
ON MAY 14, 1909

IX.—THE GARDEN OF 4 PEMBROKE VILLAS, KENSINGTON

know it is the chief road from Paris to the South & all day & all night it was one stream of fleeing refugees—Belgians—peasants from the North of France— rich Parisians—big " camions militaires " filled with wounded—autos filled with officers & soldiers. It was a fearful sight. We sat every afternoon for a couple of hours watching this stream of terrified humanity rush by.

Then suddenly the news came that all the dépôts of Fontainebleau had been evacuated in order to make room for the English army ; and that General French had established his headquarters at Melun only 20 kilometres from here. We then began arranging our house for a flight. We buried the silver & about 1000 bottles of our best wine, took all the valuable paintings down, took them off their chassis & rolled them up to take with us. I had had up to now 4 English flags on the house, & the villagers began coming & imploring me to take them down, as the Uhlans might suddenly turn up & qu'ils envoudraient plus aux anglais qu'aux français. However we only took down our flags on the morning of our departure, Saturday the 5th.

We took a train for Orléans via Malesherbes, intending to go to Nantes & then by boat to England. In Bourron we got standing room in a luggage van with 40 or 50 others & got to Malesherbes fairly quickly. There we had to wait 4 hours & at last were crowded with 60 others into a wagon à bestiaux which had just been evacuated by horses : there was at least two inches of horse droppings on the floor & we had to sit on our portmanteaus : we left Malesherbes at 5 p.m. & arrived at Orléans at 3.30 a.m., a distance of 60 kilometres. There was not a room to be had in Orléans. The station was crowded with refugees sleeping on the floor everywhere. At last we resigned ourselves to our fate & passed the rest of the night on a bench not far from the station.

When the hotels opened we luckily were able to get some café au lait at the Grand Hotel d'Orléans & the proprietor promised us the first room that should become free. This we got at night, and we both felt as if we had been saved from a great catastrophe. We determined not to quit this hotel until we were bombarded out of it & so we stayed a week & had a most interesting time & very good food & coffee & wine. At our table were several officers, so we got the news before the rest of the town. There are at least 100,000 soldiers in Orléans. Train after train of English passed thro' going to the front and the high road was one long cavalcade of English camions with supplies. By the by, the organisation of the English army is admirable & the admiration of everyone. I spoke to a wounded English soldier who had been at Mons & Charleroi : he had a bullet thro' his elbow & a shrapnel wound in the heel. He said that out of 1500 there were only 50 left. The most heartrending of all was to see the trains with wounded arrive. Only then does one realise what war is. We saw soldiers on stretchers with both legs shot off. There are 35,000 wounded now in Orléans & fresh coming night & day.

As soon as we heard of the German defeat & repulse we determined to go back to Grez & started yesterday morning at 9.50. At Malesherbes we had 7 hours to wait : & we saw a train full of German wounded come thro'. They looked awfully sick & some must have had fearful wounds as they were lying side by side in the straw. There were also 2 spies that had been taken. One was a big thickset looking German, bound hand & foot, guarded by 4 soldiers. The other was a young fellow dressed as an English soldier. I spoke to him in English but he only knew two or 3 words—he spoke French like a Frenchman. I suppose they are both dead by this time.

5

On our way from Orléans to Grez we had a first-class carriage entirely to ourselves. No one seems to be going in that direction. I shall never forget the look in the eyes of that big German spy—he seemed to know that he was already as good as dead & seemed to take no interest whatever in anything any more. Everybody, of course, wanted to have a look at him & one after the other they crowded up on to the marche pied to have a look at him—just like a menagerie. After giving a look the women generally said " Ah ! qu'il est drôle ! "

Whilst the battle of the Marne was being fought, one distinctly heard the *boum-bon-bon-boum* of the canons here in Grez. So we thought it was about time to get—as the Americans say—& not be caught in a déroute. We had of course no idea that it would be a great French victory. We can only hope now that the Allies will follow up their victory & drive the Germans home again & end this fearful carnage. If, then, the Germans will only get rid of their café concert Kaiser & his numerous family, & become a peaceable nation once more, I think there will be no more war in Europe ever again. But they've got to be smashed first—& the sooner the better.

The French have been showing qualities which I never suspected in them—a tremendous soberness & earnestness. I saw regiment upon regiment marching to the railway station on their way to the front—no military music—no tambours—silence—but every man looked in dead earnest & as if he were determined to do his best to the last.

Write to me & let me know how things are in England. Send me the D.T. war Correspondent's account of the 5 days battle of the Marne. We have begun digging up our treasures.

With love to you both from Jelka & me,—I remain yours ever,

FREDERICK DELIUS.

The Deliuses visited England in the course of 1915, and in January 1916 we find Jelka telling Adine that it is once more " so peaceful and jolly here at Grez," although their pump had broken ("really the soul of our house, as it pumps up all the water to the reservoir and from there to bath and kitchen "), and all the local *plombiers* had been called up. They were " working like niggers in the garden—doing everything ourselves, digging and pulling out weeds, cutting, planting bulbs—I am sure we shall never enjoy the garden as much as after all this work in it." But the real purpose of the letter was to ask for " news of your ' war baby.' . . . What have you done with it ? Where is it ? Fred is very interested, too, and he wants to be a god-father." When they were able to announce Yvonne's safe arrival, Jelka wrote : " How charming it really is that you have got such a lovely big baby, and a girl too, just what you wanted," and once more she declared " Fred is very eager to be god-father." Delius's christening present was a gold necklace with pearls, which he chose and bought himself.

As the war advanced into its third year, the Deliuses decided to come to England and stay in London until it ended. They had several reasons for taking this step : their financial position was complicated, for Delius (though fairly well off) had much of his money invested in Germany and America ; in London, moreover, there was not only an opportunity of hearing good music but also of having some of Delius's works performed. They were anxious, if possible, to live in a house that Balfour Gardiner then owned, in Holland Park Avenue. On January 31, 1917, Delius wrote to Norman :

GREZ-SUR-LOING (S & M).

A happy new year to you, dear old pal, & the same to Adine & the children. I was delighted to hear news from you & learn that everything is well, as far as it can be in these rotten times. If we can get Balfour's house we shall be very relieved as I hear it is difficult to hire flats or furnished houses. We are thinking of hiring a house in London & living there most of the time. I am thirsting for music & there is none here & very little even in Paris & then nothing of interest. I am making efforts to get a pass via Calais or Boulogne as I rather wish to avoid the long night passage via Havre— Southampton. They will also not allow us to bring our *bonne*, which is a great drawback, as she is so excellent. However I have appealed to my influential friends in London & am awaiting their answer.

I think England owes me a " safe conduct " by the safest & shortest route ! I am bringing 7 manuscript works with me. If I cannot get the pass, we may probably go to Switzerland for a couple of months & they will produce one or 2 of my new works there. But we are quite " en l'air " & have decided nothing—Balfour's house would probably turn the balance. I want to edit my works in London, as I now have to earn some more money. As soon as we get back our sequestered fortune we shall furnish a house in London. Is Beecham giving interesting music in London ? I shall approach him when I see him in London about my new works.

For the last 16 days we have had Arctic cold & cannot keep our house warm, as we only have wood to burn. I have just finished a new work *Eventyr* after Asbjornsen's fairy tales for orchestra & have rather tired my eyes. I am just longing for a change & *Music*.

Good-bye & au revoir I hope soon,—Ever your friend,

FREDERICK DELIUS.

In the end the Deliuses succeeded in transporting their *bonne*. Mention of the " seven manuscript works " that Delius brought with him recalls a story told by Mr. Ernest Irving :

Happy memories are still cherished in the Savage Club [Mr. Irving writes] of a famous occasion when Delius dined there, having left his trunk containing all his scores in the middle of St. Pancras station. A bodyguard of Savages, led by Norman O'Neill, conveyed the great composer, between the fish and the joint, to the station in a four-wheeler, to fetch the precious books, and were nearly impounded by the metropolitan police on the return journey. Delius had insisted that a careful eye was to be kept upon the treasure, and so O'Neill mounted beside the trunk on the roof of the cab, which brought all the Adelphi constabulary out to see the disembarkment.

Norman became a member of the Savage Club in October 1916. Hitherto he had always come home for Adine's excellent dinner between matinée and evening performances, but his varicose veins made "strap-hanging" in crowded tube trains a trying business, and one reason why he joined a club was to

Keep our house warm, as we only have wood to burn — I have just finished a new work "Eventyr" after Hans Andersens fairy tales for Orchestra & have rather tired my eyes. I am just longing for a change & Music.

Good bye & au revoir I hope soon

Love your friend

Frederick Delius

have somewhere to go for supper. He became an extremely popular member of the Savage Club, on whose committee he served for nine years. Later, he was also elected to the Beefsteak Club. At both places his cheerfulness and friendliness, and his "silvery laugh," were always welcome; for he was essentially what Dr. Johnson would have called a "clubable" man.

In 1919–20 Norman and Delius were in correspondence about the first performance of a Delius masterpiece, the *Song of the High Hills*, which had been composed eight years earlier but was not heard until February 1920, when it was conducted by Albert Coates at a Philharmonic concert. Norman was by this time treasurer of the Philharmonic Society, and was therefore asked to deal with questions such as that raised in the first paragraph of the following letter, dictated and signed by Delius in Norway in August 1919 :

DEAR NORMAN,—I have just received a letter from F. E. C. Leuckart, Salomon Str. 9, Leipsic, asking me how many Doublier Stimmen Orchestral Parts and how many Choral Parts will be required for the London performance of the *Song of the High Hills*. Please answer direct to Leuckart and at once, in order to save time. I think the later the performance takes place the better.

We are having a lovely time up in the mountains here—any amount of good things to eat, butter, milk, cream, etc., all in profusion, and heavenly air and view.

The *Uraufführung* of my last music-drama *Fennimore and Gerda* takes place in Frankfurt a/M in October, I have just heard, and in September we have to go there for the rehearsals. I have also just received news that the *Arabesque*, *Appalachia* and the *Mass of Life* are to be given in Vienna this winter. They are spending more money on music in Germany than ever. They have sent the scene *instructeur* from Frankfurt to Denmark to make studies for the scenery and *milieu* for my opera and all will be painted quite new (11 scenes). A wonderful country ! My publisher (Universal Ed. in Vienna), whom I had asked whether he suffered very much these last years, answered " Nur seelisch."

I lunched with Beecham before I left London. He is doing the *Village Romeo* in his next season ; and also *Fennimore and Gerda* next summer season.

I am having the full score of the *Song of the High Hills* sent direct to Coates, whom I saw before leaving London. We wonder where and how you are and if you are away on a holiday too. . . .

Best love to Adine and her mother and a kiss for Yvonne.

With love to you both,—Yours always,

FREDERICK DELIUS.

Fennimore and Gerda was very favourably received at its first performance in Frankfort. For the London performance of *A Song of the High Hills*, the O'Neills again asked Delius to stay at Pembroke Villas. On February 10, 1920, he wrote accepting the invitation and giving instructions as to the programme note on the work :

GREZ-SUR-LOING (S & M).

MY DEAR NORMAN,—Thanks for your letter which crossed Jelka's. I want the note on the *Song of the h. hills* to be as short & simple as possible. I have tried to express the joy & exhilaration one feels in the Mountains &

also the loneliness & melancholy of the high Solitudes & the grandeur of the wide far distances. The human voices represent man in Nature; an episode, which becomes fainter & then disappears altogether. This is very badly put & must not figure on the programme as it is—perhaps you can word it better. You know what I mean.

It is so kind of you to invite me to stay with you & I thank you both most heartily. I shall give you as little trouble as possible I hope but it will be nice to see each other again & chat a little more often. I shall arrive in London (Victoria) at 8 p.m. February 18th & shall come at once to No. 4— no doubt you will be at the theatre, so I may only see you next day. I shall have a rehearsal of the Double Concerto no doubt on the 19th or 20th.

With love to you both,—I remain yours ever,

FREDERICK DELIUS.

I shall travel via Boulogne.

Delius came alone and stayed at Pembroke Villas for a fortnight. He spent some of the time reading the script of Flecker's *Hassan*, preparatory to writing his lovely music for that play. Adine remembers that he forgot to bring his evening-dress trousers, and that when Lady Cunard asked him to join her party in their box at Covent Garden he had to wear a pair of blue trousers, which meant sitting at the back of the box and not going to a reception afterwards.

It was at this time that the first signs of Delius's eventual paralysis began to show themselves. Henceforth he wrote few letters in his own hand; but the friendly, natural and unaffected letters which have been given in the preceding pages may help to soften the legend of a stern, unapproachable Delius that has been fostered by accounts and photographs of his later years. To those who knew him in the gaiety and charm of his prime, the emphasis given to those years of disability after the age of sixty has seemed disproportionate, and even in writing of his last years too much stress can hardly be laid on the courage with which he faced paralysis, pain and blindness, and continued to compose.

Jelka Delius's letters to the O'Neills during the 1920's show clearly how this devoted woman sacrificed herself for her husband; they would be an invaluable source of information for the definitive biography of Delius which has yet to be written. There are many references to the difficulties experienced by Delius in obtaining his income from foreign investments and his royalties from music publishers. Delius lived internationally rather than nationally; and his English birth, French residence, German ancestry, and American and Norwegian associations, all made his finances extremely complicated. Thus, in the summer of 1922, when Delius's illness seriously declared itself, and doctors' fees and treatment at Wiesbaden and Wildbad began to eat up money, we find Mrs. Delius writing to Adine :

Our finances are of course the great source of anxiety for us both. And I do hope and wish you would do all you can to have his works performed. It is his 60th birthday on the 29th of Jan. and Dr. Simon is writing a short biography with some splendid etchings of Fred which is to be brought out by Piper in Munich. . . . For that occasion they wish to arrange a Delius concert at Frankfort. . . . Could not the Philharmonic also give a Delius concert ? . . . They might do *Sea Drift* with the Philharmonic Choir. The *'Cello Concerto* will also be ready by then. The *Double Concerto* is out now (score and all). *North Country Sketches* will also be ready at Augeners. The *Arabesque* (baritone solo and chorus and orch.) has never been given in London, and no end of other things. Of course Fred does not know I am writing this, and *must never know*. But something in the way of a boom must be done, otherwise *how shall we live* ? What we get from German publishers is practically worthless now. . . .

Jelka explained that Delius had not had a stroke or seizure, but " rather a physical breakdown, mentally he is as fresh and vivacious as ever, but his legs and arms are so very weak." With difficulty he was taken that summer from Wildbad to a hut in Gudbrandsdalen in Norway which had just been built to their design. He was encouraged to try to play a little each day, and a piano was hired in Christiania and hauled up the steep hillside to the hut by two horses, who had first experimented with the kitchen stove. " I shall try to get him to write a little dance for Yvonne," said Jelka.

On August 20, 1922, Delius dictated the following letter :

HOIFAGERLI (the name of our hut),
LESJASKOG, GUDBRANDSDALEN.

(Jelka, amanuensis).

DEAR NORMAN,—Since the end of June we have been up in our hut in the high mountains and altho' the weather has been wet and cold lately our stay is a great success ; we love our hut which is beautifully built and in a lovely situation. I am walking about with 2 sticks now out of doors and with one stick in the rooms, which is quite a great improvement, and I hope my legs and arms will continue to get stronger gradually.

Would the Philharmonic like to give the 1st performance of my *'Cello Concerto* with Beatrice Harrison ? Perhaps in March ? Universal Edition is publishing it and I have just corrected the proofs of the full score and piano score. Why not give the *Song of the High Hills* again with that lovely Kennedy Scott chorus ? And why not *Paris* ? It has not been heard for a long time in London. All these belong now to the Universal Edition, Vienna, Karlsplatz 6.

Please tell Adine that I have just written a little prelude for Yvonne for her album and will send it to her in a few days. We leave Kristiania for Grez on Sept. 9th.

With love to you both,—Affly. yours, FREDERICK DELIUS.

Apparently he was not quite satisfied that his little prelude was the best he could do for his god-daughter, for in March 1923 Jelka wrote to Adine :

I posted seven little piano pieces to you yesterday. Fred wants me to tell you that he composed them, each one, so as to make an easy piece for Yvonne, but they always grew too difficult, but the seventh one, we think, is quite easy ; should anything be too wide stretched for her hands, it can be arranged by giving it to the other hand, I think.

Fred is rather diffident about the pieces and begs you to see if you think *all* of them should be published, or some left back. He leaves it to you to see. They are my début as an amanuensis, as he cannot write and has to dictate it all to me and I find it pretty difficult. . . .

The endless search for health continued. In 1923 the Deliuses stayed at Frankfort (where Percy Grainger was with them) and at Bad Oeynhausen, in Westphalia, before going to Norway. The next year Delius was taken to Cassel for treatment. Another time he went to Rapallo. ("This house is rather uncomfortable. . . . There are 56 very steep stone steps leading up through the garden. Then there is another stone staircase in the house to lead to the bedrooms. Fred cannot walk any of this, and we have to carry him up and down.") Now and then there would be a little improvement in his condition, but, as Jelka said, it was a " long, weary way " ; and it did him no good, of course, to worry about money and about publishers and copyright societies who did not pay up at the proper time and rate. In such cases Norman's services were in request as mediator :

. . . I know you are frightfully busy, dear Norman, but if you could just have a talk with them and get them to tip up it would be a real act of friendship. We are spending a lot of money here [Cassel], and we have a trained nurse now ; it all costs a lot. . . .

The one great comfort was that Delius's music was at last obtaining world-wide recognition :

I am so delighted Beecham gave *In a Summer Garden* [wrote Jelka in January, 1926]. Did I tell you that the *Mass of Life* was given on December 18 with greatest success at Coblenz, on February 4 it will be done at Hagen, later on at Duisburg and in May in Wiesbaden and Frankfurt. The *Song of the High Hills* is down for performance in Athens—*Sea Drift* at Gotha—*Paris* was just done in Vienna. . . .

By 1927 hopes of any permanent recovery had waned ; but the indomitable man was nevertheless " not doing too badly, he is eating oysters all the time and that seems always to do him good. . . ."

The pastel portrait of Delius at the age of thirty, now reproduced for the first time, came into Adine's possession, through the generosity of Balfour Gardiner, after Delius's death ; but it had been in the O'Neills' house before, for Jelka, writing in 1928, says :

. . . It is so kind of you to keep Fred's pastel portrait. It always had a few small damp spots—but maybe they have increased. I am very fond of it. The hands and whole pose was very like him at the time. It is painted by Daniel de Monfreid, the friend of Gauguin. . . .

The O'Neills also bore a share of responsibility for another Delius portrait—that painted by James Gunn and exhibited at the Royal Academy in 1933—for it was Norman who persuaded Delius to allow Gunn to paint him.

The last letter from Delius to Norman that has been preserved was dictated to Jelka on April 24, 1929, not long after he had been made a Companion of Honour :

GREZ-SUR-LOING.

Fred dictates.

DEAR NORMAN,—It was very nice of you to send those cuttings. I only wish they would do *Hassan* again. As to the C.H., I should very much like to know what Newman replied. There are many people who hint that the C.H. is not very much. It would seem strange, of course, if they had given me a lesser honour than to musicians like Landon Ronald, Edw. German, Ham. Harty, etc. !

Mr. Nevile Henderson, the British Minister plenipotentiary in Paris, came here last Sunday to hand me the decoration.

Please try to find out how it really is ! We shall love to have you come here on a visit as soon and *when* you like.

The tailor you recommended me has made me a very good dark blue serge suit. I have just ordered another pair of trousers and an overcoat, for which latter I have sent him an old one that was very agreeable, as a pattern for cut, stuff and thickness. I hope he will imitate it alright. Jelka has written him all details.

Well, old friend ! Do come soon,—Ever affly.

FR. DELIUS.

Mrs. Delius added as a postscript :

Much love from Jelka. Fred has just made a glorious orchestral suite with chorus of the *Hassan* music, with the aid of Eric Fenby.

Eric Fenby had lately arrived at Grez to take up his work as Delius's amanuensis, which was to give new interest to the composer's life, and of which he has left a fascinating description in *Delius as I Knew Him*. The following lines from Fenby's book were written with reference to the visit by Norman hinted at in Delius's letter ; they will make a fitting close to this chapter :

Our next visitor was that charming and genial Irishman, Norman O'Neill. Delius had already spoken of him with the greatest affection, and when they were together I could see that O'Neill was one of the very few people whom he loved. That impersonal, almost indifferent attitude which characterised most of his human relationships left him completely whenever mention was made of O'Neill, and when I think of the way in which he looked forward to O'Neill's yearly visits, and the delight with which he relished his friend's amusing accounts of the latest happenings in London— for the old man always smacked his lips over a bit of good, honest gossip— it is not strange that I can rarely think of O'Neill without hearing in my mind that unaccustomed friendliness which would creep into Delius's voice as he said, "Norman is coming," or, "I've heard from Norman this morning." It was as if he had suddenly returned to the level of the normal balance of mankind. All the nervous tension and sense of detachment that surrounded him, and made him so difficult and inaccessible, save on rare occasions, vanished with these words.

. . . O'Neill was devoted to Delius, though not blindly. Of all men, he knew his Delius the man just as well as he knew his Delius the composer. He told me that Fred's music meant more to him than the work of any composer, past or present.

I, for one, will always remember him with gratitude, for without his moral support and advice the difficulties with which I had to contend at Grez as time went on would have been too much for me. He understood everything.

CHAPTER X

TREASURER OF THE "PHIL"

HAVING reached the year 1916, we broke off our account of Norman's life in order to consider his friendship with Delius, and we now resume it in the same year.

It was a great honour to Norman to be asked to open the tercentenary Shakespeare celebrations at Drury Lane, on May 2, 1916, by conducting his "Hamlet" overture. His fellow-conductors in a concert of Shakespearean music were Henry Wood, Hamilton Harty, Sir A. Mackenzie, Thomas Beecham and Edward German. Then came a performance of *Julius Cæsar*, with Henry Ainley as Antony, Frank Benson as Cæsar, and H. B. Irving as Cassius. The King and Queen were present, and Frank Benson was knighted on that afternoon—the first time that any actor had been knighted in a theatre. Norman took something of a family interest in the ceremony, for the new knight had often played with him and his brothers in their nursery at Young Street, long ago, and Frank Benson's brother Cecil had married his sister Constance.

The services of musicians and actors were given free on this occasion, to the honour of Shakespeare and to the profit of the Red Cross. Between 1914 and 1918 Norman several times contributed to performances in aid of war charities, twice writing music to scripts by Monckton Hoffe. One of these, performed at the Chelsea Palace, was a short sketch called "the Rossetti Scene," in which the ghosts of Rossetti, Meredith, Morris, Carlyle, and others, met at midnight in a Chelsea garden. The other was more ambitious : it was a Swinburne ballet, *Before Dawn*, danced by Madame Astafieva and students of her school at a matinée at the Lyric Theatre on June 29, 1917, in aid of Lena Ashwell's "Concerts at the Front."

For this ballet Monckton Hoffe wrote a story of a jealous king and a dancing girl, of a virtuous wife and her passionate lover, on the theme of Swinburne's lines :

> For a day and a night Love sang to us, played with us,
> Folded us round from the dark and the light. . . .

The Swinburne stanzas were recited before the opening of the ballet, and a chorus of women's voices was employed during it.

Norman's music, said *The Times*, was " crisp and to the point " ; the dance was " long enough to test a composer's powers," but he " did not repeat himself and the interest was not allowed to flag." The ballet ran for several weeks at the Coliseum, and on September 29, 1917, Norman conducted the music at a Promenade Concert at the Queen's Hall.

There was an air raid on London that Saturday night. *Before Dawn* was given without disturbance, but after the interval, when Carmen Hill was singing, ominous sounds were heard outside. During the next item, a bassoon solo, there came a crash and a cracking sound, and a shower of plaster fell from the roof of the Promenade. The audience was rather alarmed, but Henry Wood continued to conduct (though he looked up anxiously at the ceiling) and the bassoonist, Wilfred James, kept on playing. After the concert no one was allowed to leave until 1.0 a.m., and Adine invited the youngest member of the Oriana Choir—which had undertaken the voice part of *Before Dawn*— to stay the night at Pembroke Villas, because she had a long way to go home.

Trivial though such incidents were, in comparison with the raid of 1941 which destroyed the Queen's Hall, Norman nevertheless found the air raids of 1917 rather trying to his nerves, and in March 1918 he decided to give himself a holiday from them, and rented a house at Shere for six months. His daughter Yvonne's first memory of her father is of being pushed by him, at the age of two, in a wheelbarrow down to the White Horse to fetch a barrel of beer ; linked with this, is an impression of a famous Shere inhabitant, H. B. Marriott Watson—the novelist, and collaborator with Barrie in an early play,—very large and very red, with a big black hat and a chow dog.

At Shere Norman enrolled as a stretcher-bearer and met trains of wounded that arrived at the railway station. His song " Eagles of England," dedicated to the R.A.F., was published in 1918 ; and while at Shere he wrote some martial and patriotic music for a play called *Freedom* which was produced by Lyall Swete in New York in the same year. More characteristic was the exquisite incidental music he composed at Shere for Maud V. Vernon's fairy play, *Through the Green Door*, produced at the Gaiety Theatre, Manchester, at Christmas 1919. Years later Miss Vernon wrote to Adine that her play " owed everything to his very beautiful music (one day, I trust, to be heard with it again)." *Through ·the Green Door* was a delightful play which deserved to succeed, but it never came to London. Six songs from it were published, however, and Norman made a suite out of the music. Another fairy play for which he wrote music, *A Poor Little Rich Girl*, suffered a similar fate.

In the autumn of 1918 the O'Neills returned to London, and for some time Norman took over the orchestra of St. Paul's Girls' School, while Gustav Holst was away on a tour organising music for the troops in Salonika and Asia Minor. But the closing years of the war were chiefly memorable in Norman's life for the new responsibilities he now accepted in connection with the Royal Philharmonic Society, of which he became honorary co-treasurer in 1916 and honorary treasurer in 1918.

He was peculiarly adapted to render full service to the " Phil." To him was entrusted the choice of the players forming what was then known as the " Royal Philharmonic Orchestra." No one was better fitted for this task, as he knew the value of every orchestral player in London ; and as a result of his wise selection the Philharmonic was for many years one of the finest orchestras ever heard. His tact and firmness were invaluable in time of difficulty—such as a difference with certain orchestral players about the " deputy system "—and his own standing as an artist made him an ideal person to receive and deal with the great artists who came to the " Phil."

Mr. J. Mewburn Levien, for many years secretary of the Royal Philharmonic Society, contributed the following appreciation to *The Times* after Norman's death :

The debt which it has been said every man owes to the profession by which he lives has never been more generously acknowledged and handsomely paid than by Norman O'Neill. While never neglecting the proper marketing of his abilities and genius—and there was a constant and competitive demand for the whole of his output—O'Neill found a surprising amount of time for voluntary work on the committee of the Savage Club and the direction of the Royal Philharmonic Society. As regards the latter institution, it would be difficult to over-value his services. His knowledge of music, breadth of view in regard to it, friendship with practically all the men of light and leading in the world of his art, care for the claims of British music, intimate acquaintance with everything that concerned the orchestra, technical and personal, power of estimating soloists, sensing the views of various groups of music-lovers, and adjusting programmes so as to meet them, with due regard to the financial position and the part the society was expected to play in the national life, all these O'Neill had in a marked degree, and he exercised them with a swiftness of apprehension and a firmness of purpose which won the admiration of his colleagues.

As an artist of Irish origin O'Neill had naturally not too much inborn love of rules and regulations for their own sake. Nevertheless, he recognised in a way unfortunately not always found with genius-endowed folk that work for a society is best done, and duty demands that it should be done, within the framework of its constitution. If, however, a new interpretation had to be given to an old rule or the time had come to take an adventure into the unknown, no one entered on the task with greater spirit and more cheerful humour than O'Neill. In this connection the great proportion of contemporary and especially English contemporary music produced by the society of late years [before 1934], and the adaptation of the " Old Phil " to the successive eras of the gramophone, the B.B.C. and Sir Thomas Beecham, keeping its own course, but working with all, may be cited. It is not too much indeed to say that many a page of interesting reading in the history of music in England in the last quarter of a century would have been a blank but for O'Neill. His handsome presence, constant friendliness and helpfulness, delightful conversation, and authoritative ways, will long be missed by an unusually wide circle.

In 1919 Schott published Norman's three Old English pieces for piano, and Ascherberg his " Carillon " (op. 50, 2), which was also published in Braille. This last appeared in a series of pianoforte music by modern British composers, including Stanford, Ireland and Bax. In the autumn of 1919 Norman temporarily left the Haymarket to go to the St. James's Theatre, where Henry Ainley was making his debut as actor-manager, in association with Gilbert Miller. Norman and Ainley had known each other since the days of *A Tragedy of Truth*, and they were now close friends ; at the age of six, Norman's daughter Yvonne was entrusted to the Ainleys for a fortnight, at their house near Sevenoaks.

The play chosen to open Ainley's London management was *Reparation* (Tolstoy's *The Living Corpse*), which, for all its queernesses and faults of construction, made an interesting evening. Ainley and Marion Terry gave admirable performances as the waster Fedya and as Anna Karenin. Norman arranged some Russian gipsy songs and folk music for *Reparation*, and the songs (translated by A. Kalisch) and a waltz were published in the same year.

The main purpose of Norman's visit to the St. James's, however, was to write music for his third Shakespeare play, *Julius Cæsar*, in which Ainley repeated the fine performance as Mark Antony which he had given at Drury Lane in 1916. The music was highly thought of, and, with Basil Gill and Milton Rosmer, the production proved a notable success. Norman took some words from " Lucrece " for the song of Lucius, with its " sleepy tune," which Master George Hamilton piped in a natural, boyish way in Brutus's tent. The producer was Colonel Stanley Bell, an old friend of Norman since the days when he had been stage-manager of His Majesty's under Sir Herbert Tree.

Julius Cæsar ran from the beginning of January 1920 until the end of March, when a light comedy brought Henry Ainley's season to a close. But in the meantime the Haymarket management had sent Norman the script of a new play by J. M. Barrie, *Mary Rose*, which they had decided to produce in the spring. They felt that this was a play that simply cried out for music, and that no one could be better fitted than Norman to write it.

CHAPTER XI

" MARY ROSE "—AND AFTER

ALTHOUGH Norman was immediately gripped by *Mary Rose*, and fully realised its musical possibilities, Sir James Barrie was doubtful at first whether music was necessary, or would be a help in getting the atmosphere and effects he wanted. However, as soon as Barrie had heard Norman's music at a special audition, he liked it, and his liking increased at the rehearsals. He did not at first seem the most encouraging of authors to work for, as Thomas Hardy's description of him at one of the rehearsals of *Mary Rose* indicates :

> If any day a promised play
> Should be in preparation,
> You never see friend J. M. B.
> Depressed or in elation.
> But with a stick, rough, crooked and thick,
> You may sometimes discern him,
> Standing as though a mummery show
> Did not at all concern him.

Yet Barrie was really most anxiously concerned about the whole production, and eventually showed his appreciation of Norman's music as emphatically as possible, by describing its effect in the published version of *Mary Rose*, and thus virtually incorporating it into his play.

Barrie's original idea of the disappearance of Mary Rose can be seen in the typescript of the play which is preserved at the Haymarket Theatre. His stage directions at the end of Act II read :

> The island has begun to " call " to Mary Rose. . . . The sound is soon like a great storm of waves and screaming winds, whose effects may possibly be best got musically but perhaps best by stage mechanism. . . .

And a few lines further on :

> . . . The storm suddenly ceases. There are two seconds' silence, and then a dreadful tearing sound is heard as if something in Nature were being rent in two—then again stillness. . . .

Holman Clark, the producer, spent the greater part of one morning in the orchestra pit making weird noises to represent the " dreadful tearing sound," and ingenious mechanical tricks were experimented with for the disappearance. One of these

X.—DELIUS AT THE AGE OF THIRTY

From a hitherto unpublished pastel portrait by Daniel de Monfreid, dated
February 1893, now in the possession of Mrs. Norman O'Neill.

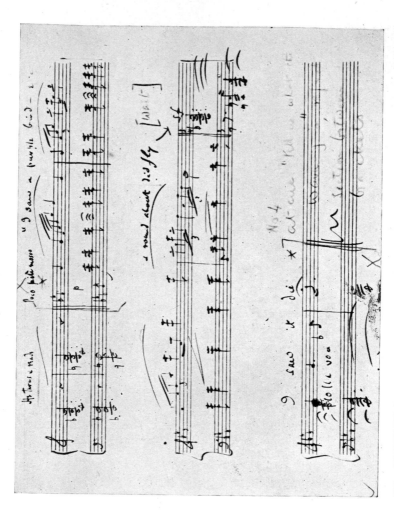

XI.—EXCERPT FROM NORMAN O'NEILL'S OWN PIANO ARRANGEMENT FROM
THE SCORE OF *THE GOLDEN DOOM*

was an arrangement of mirrors, which made Mary Rose disappear most satisfactorily so far as the stalls were concerned, but unfortunately left her in full view from the gallery. As soon as Norman's music had been heard it was realised that none of this mechanism was necessary, and that the best course was simply to make Mary Rose walk off the stage, entranced, while the music, and the women's voices calling through it, did the rest.

Thus, in the printed version of the play, the stage direction became :

The call has come to Mary Rose. It is at first as soft and furtive as whisperings from holes in the ground, "Mary Rose, Mary Rose." Then in a fury as of storm and whistling winds that might be an unholy organ it rushes upon the island, raking every bush for her. These sounds increase rapidly in volume till the mere loudness of them is horrible. They are not without an opponent. Struggling through them, and also calling her name, is to be heard music of an unearthly sweetness that is seeking perhaps to beat them back and put a girdle of safety round her. . . .

Again, at the end of Act III, Barrie in his original typescript writes of " the same wave-sounds and winds . . . now sweet and seductive," while in the printed play the passage reads :

The call is again heard, but there is in it now no unholy sound. It is a celestial music that is calling for Mary Rose, Mary Rose, first in whispers and soon so loudly that, for one who can hear, it is the only sound in the world. Mary Rose, Mary Rose. . . . The smallest star shoots down for her, and with her arms stretched forth to it trustingly she walks out through the window into the empyrean. The music passes with her. . . .

Both these passages of Barrie are very fair descriptions of the effect of Norman's music, as anyone who cares to read them to the accompaniment of the H.M.V. recordings can testify. The stage direction at the end of Act II has been selected by Mr. Thomas Moult as being specially praiseworthy in Barrie's dramatic work, and it is interesting to note, as Mr. W. A. Darlington points out in his book on Barrie, that " it turns out not to be Barrie's work at all, but merely his description of O'Neill's work."

Norman wanted the music he had written for Mary Rose's disappearance to start with a mysterious rumble from below, in the distance ; he did not want a definite note and he thought a 32-foot organ-pipe would give the effect he aimed at. When he consulted his friend Mewburn Levien, who was interested in an organ-building business, Levien suggested that a 16-foot pipe and an 8-foot pipe, a flat fourth above, would be better, and moreover would not be such a nuisance behind the scenes. This idea was adopted, and Levien planted the two pipes on a " shop-soiled " small bellows which he found at his works. The

6

contraption cost little and worked admirably, giving just the weird effect that Norman intended. Levien formally " opened " it in the presence of Norman and of Barrie himself.

The " Call " at the end of Act II was the theme on which Norman based his music :

a theme which occurred at times cheerfully (as between the scenes of Act I and before the curtain rose on Act II) ; at other times sadly and mysteriously ; and at last in music of real beauty and serenity. Besides the two organ pipes, he used in his orchestra five violins, two violas, two violoncellos, contrabasso, oboe, flute, clarinet, harp, piano, three women's voices, and a saw !

And so we come to the first night, on April 22, 1920, of the production that Frederick Harrison, manager of the Haymarket, called " the proudest achievement of my career." Fay Compton gave perhaps the best performance of her life as Mary Rose ; Ernest Thesiger as Cameron, the Scots ghillie, was unforgettable ; and the other parts were safe in the hands of such actors as Robert Loraine, Jean Cadell and Mary Jerrold. Barrie now had nothing but praise for the music, and towards the end of the piece, when he was wandering round with his pipe, he came into the orchestra pit and very generously remarked, " Well, O'Neill, I think we've made a success." In her reminiscences Fay Compton was equally generous : " Mary Rose sang to Norman O'Neill and inspired him to write that beautiful, haunting music which in turn inspired us ; the tremendous debt of gratitude I owed to that music I can never hope to repay."

Writing to H. B. Marriott Watson on May 21, 1920, Barrie said, " I hope you will think O'Neill's music is beautiful, as I do. And a delightful man to work with too " ; and after the music had been published by Schott he wrote to Norman :

ADELPHI TERRACE HOUSE, STRAND, W.C. 2,
21 *June* 1920.

DEAR O'NEILL,—Many thanks for the copy of the music. I have been long in writing you, but the music itself lies on my table like a bowl of flowers, which indeed it is. It was a lucky day for me when you had that inspiration, and I am confident that America will acclaim it as much as they are doing here,—Yours sincerely,

J. M. BARRIE.

Mary Rose was produced in New York the following December, with Ruth Chatterton in the leading part. The first-night audience was enthusiastic, but some of the more matter-of-fact critics were not so pleased ; one of them wrote that " the play ends with the apparition seated flabbergasted on the Tommy's knee, talking airy nothings." As Denis Mackail has put it : " In America there was rather too much natural speculation as to what it was all about." Yet there was a run of 127 performances, followed by a fairly successful tour.

The 399 performances at the Haymarket were almost a record for a Barrie play. People came to see *Mary Rose* twenty or thirty times, but there were some odd misconceptions about the music. W. H. Leverton says in his reminiscences that a lady once came to his box-office window and said " I want two stalls not too near the orchestra." She was offered seats some rows back. " That's not very near the band, is it ? " she asked. " No, not very near." " Oh, well, I'll take them, thank you ; then we shan't be able to hear the din."

" Din ! " exclaims Mr. Leverton. " Norman O'Neill's lovely music ! "

There have been revivals at the Haymarket in 1926 and 1929, and several successful English tours, for two of which Leslie Bridgewater conducted the music. Norman took a keen interest in the fortunes of his music on tour, and insisted on reports from Bridgewater each week as to how the music was going, whether he could get the necessary extra players at the different towns, and so on, to all of which Norman replied with vigorous advice as to how to obtain respectable performances.

A few years later, after Norman had provided music for other Barrie plays, the Savage Club thought that it would be pleasant to see author and composer together, as guest and host, at one of the annual dinners of the club. Norman wrote to Barrie, who sent a typical reply :

ADELPHI TERRACE HOUSE, STRAND, W.C. 2,
23 Sep. 1925.

DEAR O'NEILL,—Thank you heartily for your invitation to the Savage Club annual dinner. I am very pleased to be asked but those big affairs are against the grain with me and so I must ask you to excuse me. What I should like though is to be asked to one of the Saturday dinners at the club itself, some time when your duties elsewhere wouldn't prevent your being my host. Please manage this if you can. All best regards,—Yours sincerely,

J. M. BARRIE.

But there is no record of Barrie having attended a Savage Club " Saturday night " with Norman in the chair.

The collaboration between the two over *Mary Rose* had been particularly happy. We have seen that Barrie appreciated the help that Norman's music gave to his play, and to Norman it

ADELPHI TERRACE HOUSE,

STRAND, W.C. 2.

21 June. 1920

Dear O'Neill.

Many thanks for the copy of the music. I have been long in writing you, but the music itself lies on my table like a bed of flowers, which indeed it is. It was a lovely joy for the show you had that inspiration and I am confident that music will condemn it as much as they are doing here. Yours sincerely

J. M. Barrie

meant much to be associated with a piece that, according to many critics, is Barrie's masterpiece. The *Mary Rose* music greatly increased Norman's already considerable reputation in the theatre. The "Prelude" and "Call" were first given a concert performance by Sir Henry Wood at Queen's Hall in

1921, and they have been much played since, especially on the wireless.

Of all the letters of congratulation he received, probably none pleased Norman more than the following :

> 5, HALL ROAD, ST. JOHN'S WOOD, N.W.
> *Octr. 23rd, 1920.*
>
> DEAR MR. O'NEILL,—I have just been to see *Mary Rose* & cannot refrain from writing to tell you how much I enjoyed the music. It is *most* appropriate and artistic, & creates just the right atmosphere—indeed it is a great asset to the delightful play.
>
> With my kind regards,—I am yours sincerely,
>
> EDWARD GERMAN.

Mary Rose was by no means an isolated activity of the year 1920. Norman was soon engaged in composing music for a production of *Macbeth*, which opened at the Aldwych Theatre on November 2, with the American James K. Hackett as Macbeth and Mrs. Patrick Campbell as Lady Macbeth. This was Hackett's favourite part, and he gave, as usual, a very sound and competent performance, albeit one " more notably sensible and intelligible than contemplative and lyrical," as *The Times* remarked. The French government thereupon invited him to play Macbeth in English in Paris, and he did so with success in the following year, Sybil Thorndike playing Lady Macbeth.

In 1920 Augener published Norman's orchestration of Coleridge-Taylor's " Three-Fours " suite ; in 1921 Schott published his " Celtic Legend " and " Nocturne " for violin and piano, and in 1922 his *entr'acte* " Running Water." Two plays for which, perhaps rather unexpectedly, he wrote music at this time were *The Knave of Diamonds* (from which a suite was published) and *The Way of an Eagle*, both adaptations of novels by Ethel M. Dell. Neither play had a long run ; but Ethel M. Dell was then in her best-seller's hey-day, and police were needed to protect her from the mobs of young women who swarmed out-side the stage-doors of the Globe and the Adelphi. Her admirers were rewarded by a glimpse of a refined, schoolmistress-like lady, very quiet and shy.

Norman composed the song, "Yo-ho-ho and a Bottle of Rum," which Charles Hawtrey sang in *Ambrose Applejohn's Adventure* in 1921. He also wrote music for *The Love Thief*, the melodrama adapted from the Italian by C. B. Fernald, produced in September 1921, with Norman McKinnel and Cathleen Nesbitt. More to his taste, however, was the revival at the Haymarket of Barrie's *Quality Street*, which followed the long run of *Mary Rose*. The war of 1914–18 had given new point and attraction to a play which had been first performed in 1902, and Fay Compton as Phœbe Throssel (the original Phœbe, Ellaline Terriss, threw her a bouquet at the first night), and Leon Quartermaine as Valentine Brown carried *Quality Street* through a triumphant run of 344 performances, from August 1921 to June 1922, an unusually fortunate revival. Norman was now firmly reinstalled in his old post at the Haymarket, and his much-reduced orchestra still kept up, by its qualities, the reputation gained in former years. For *Quality Street* he made some delightful arrangements (published by Schott) of old dances—including minuets, a gavotte and a quadrille—from Corelli, Lully, Handel and traditional airs.

To round off two busy years, he composed music for a ballet, *The Snow Queen*, founded on Hans Andersen's story. It was one of the most attractive items in Marian Wilson's season of British ballet at the Kingsway in October and November 1921.

Let us pause for a moment to take a longer view of Norman's work in the theatre. No one is better fitted to give a critic's opinion than Mr. Francis Toye, for many years music critic of *Vanity Fair* and *The Morning Post* ; and no one within the musical profession is more qualified to assess Norman's achievement than Mr. Ernest Irving, who has himself written the music for many plays and served as musical director of most of the West-End theatres.

Mr. Francis Toye has obligingly supplied the author with the following estimate :

Essentially the man of the theatre, Norman O'Neill was ready to turn out incidental music to order at any time. His technique in this respect was very remarkable. He knew all the dodges : optional repeats of 4 or 8 bars, tremolandos of indefinite duration, and so on. Moreover he was an expert in getting the maximum of variety and sonority out of the necessarily exiguous theatre orchestra, knowing the precise quality and capacity of every instrument in every position. For these reasons he was almost the ideal theatre musician, practical, experienced as no one else. But at times his music rose superior to this effectiveness, this unerring sense of the right phrase in the right place, which were his hall-mark. Most people would consider his incidental music to *The Blue Bird* or *Mary Rose* the high-water mark of his achievement. That, however, is a mistake. The best music O'Neill wrote was for Lord Dunsany's plays, for here the fantasy and imagination of the subject-matter was perfectly matched, and enhanced, by the fantasy and imagination of his really beautiful music.

Having read what Mr Toye has written, Mr. Ernest Irving writes :

Mr. Francis Toye's appreciation of Norman O'Neill's work in the theatre is external and critical, as befits a critic. Though O'Neill did understand

the theatre and its music as well as any professional music director of his
time, it should not be supposed that composition with him was a mental
process to be compared with that which actuates the property master or the
costumier. What made his theatre music more effective than that of his
contemporaries was not only its theatrical fitness but its dramatic content,
and it was by no means principally, or even largely, composed of "dodges."

Before accepting a commission to write incidental music, O'Neill insisted
upon the fullest conference with the author, producer, and all connected with
the artistic side of the play ; including occasionally the actors and actresses
who had to sing his songs without possessing the necessary natural qualifications for such work. He sought and accepted advice from disinterested
friends, and laboured anxiously to give of his very best so far as the demands
of occasional music allowed him. To say that he was expert in getting the
maximum of variety and sonority out of the "necessarily exiguous" theatre
orchestra is to put it too low ; one would not say that Mozart and Brahms
did very well with their material in the clarinet quintets. O'Neill was a
master of scoring for small combinations, and I do not think he would have
wished to have his *Mary Rose* music played by a larger or better orchestra
than the one he employed at the Haymarket—about 18 players.

In order to fit "background music" behind dialogue it is of primary
importance, of course, not to shackle the actor, who may, and probably
should, vary his performance from night to night, hence the optional repeat
and indefinite tremolando ; but the background music of O'Neill contained
a latent subconscious potency which was frequently of the utmost value in
colouring, emphasising and illustrating the inflexions of the speech behind
which, so unobtrusively, it was played. He was a past master in artistic
economy, and knew better than any man I have met what not to do and
what to excise. His Shakespearean music was contrived, where it accompanied speech, to run in double harness with the dialogue, and was full of
tiny and subtle effects which were all the more effective in that they were
suggestive without being assertive.

I do consider that *Mary Rose* was the high-water mark of his achievement
in the theatre, because it used music as a bridge between the human and the
supernatural ; and in my opinion, a performance of *Mary Rose* without
O'Neill's music is like a dance by a fairy with a wooden leg. The cunning
way in which the voices were blended with the orchestral texture, the use of
an enormous pedal diapason organ pipe, emitting a sound which could be
sensed by the audience rather than heard, and the sweet reasonableness of
the mellifluous sound which accompanied the hair-raising episode of Mary
Rose's disappearance from "The Island that Liked to be Visited," were all
points of a major experiment in the magical. Not all O'Neill's theatre music
was as successful as this. The experiment of voices in the orchestra was
repeated in his setting of *Macbeth* with less successful result, and when he
supplied the score of an ordinary melodrama he was known, at times, to fit
it with the music it deserved.

He was very popular with all stage people who were associated with
his music, because of his charming personality and apparent deference to
their wishes ; but he could be fiery and unmoveable when the music was
really threatened with damage, and I have seen him fight a battle royal with
a producer over a completely non-musical issue, in which his unerring
dramatic instinct served him well. Many actors are completely ignorant of
music and all its ways, and to such he had a genial address in the style of

the principal of a successful Kindergarten. He cured a certain famous actress who demanded a pibroch in *Macbeth* by writing one which he alleged was to accompany the "sleep-walking scene." This completely frightened the lady, who fell feebly back upon the demand for a musical owl to hoot before the murder scene. O'Neill regretted that the only person that he knew who could imitate an owl was playing the lead in a musical comedy, and was not disengaged, so the property man came into his own again.

The timing of the music at the Haymarket was achieved by the aid of a wonderful system of electric lights, which anticipated by many years the appearance of the traffic lights in Piccadilly Circus; but lights would have been useless without the co-operative, controlling hands of Charles La Trobe and Stanley Bell. In them he found the only two men in London who could be trusted to work a musical score from the switchboard.

O'Neill's tremendous success with *Mary Rose* placed him above criticism, and brought him a large number of offers from managements anxious to build up bad plays with good music. He had to have, however, some sympathy with the work before he could give it suitable music, and on the few occasions in which he concerned himself with inferior plays, such as, for instance, *The Way of an Eagle*, his work was second class. It was, nevertheless, accepted by his grateful purchasers as if it had been written by Beethoven.

I believe O'Neill himself liked his Shakespearean music best, and there was a tremendous amount of musical thought in his scores for *Hamlet, Julius Cæsar, Henry V,* and perhaps best of all, *The Merchant of Venice,* which in some curious way gave a genuine Venetian atmosphere to the play. He was most modest about his compositions, and his interests lay heart and soul in good music. I served with him for nearly twenty years on the committee of the Royal Philharmonic Society and the amount of labour and thought that he gave to his work on behalf of good music was stupendous, considering what a busy life his was. He knew all the composers, conductors, pianists and violinists in Europe, and a great number of the singers too.

O'Neill did much to lift the standard of small band *entr'acte* music by scoring a number of little, unknown semi-classics for the excellent players he employed at the Haymarket Theatre. One could frequently hear during the *entr'acte* Purcell, Corelli, Vivaldi and other seventeenth and eighteenth century composers, given careful hearing by an audience who in other theatres would be found, between the acts, in other places. He always managed to find *entr'acte* music that fitted both the play and the theatre.

He was a true and kind friend to a great number of musicians and was always exerting himself to find theatre work for members of the symphony orchestras who had too much spare time upon their hands. His boundless good-nature, unfailing sense of humour and kindness of heart to musicians of all kinds gave him a very extensive circle of friends who must still miss the well-loved personality. His departure made a hole in my life which has never been quite filled up.

CHAPTER XII

BELASCO'S " MERCHANT OF VENICE "

APART from Martin-Harvey's *Hamlet*, Norman had already
written incidental music for two plays produced in New York—
A Lonely Queen and *Freedom*; but the success of the *Mary Rose* music
greatly increased his American reputation and he now accepted
an invitation from David Belasco to write music for *The Merchant
of Venice*, which he was producing in the autumn of 1922, and
to go over to New York to supervise the musical side of the
production. He arranged to stay for a few weeks, on his way
to New York, with his American friends, Mr. and Mrs. Avery
Robinson, at their house at Forest Nook, Ontario. The music
was completed in such good time that on June 14, 1922, he was
able to conduct a performance of five of the Preludes by the
Harrogate Municipal Orchestra at the Royal Hall, Harrogate.

But when the time approached for departure, he did not at
all want to go. He always hated leaving England, and, despite
his naval godfather, he had acquired a dislike of the sea and
especially of being on it. To Adine, who was on holiday at Le
Touquet with Yvonne, he wrote : " I cannot say I feel ' cheerful '
as the day draws nearer ; but, as you say, I may like it after all
when I get there ! " And on August 30 : " I have been packing !
a melancholy proceeding. I wish you were here to help me, but
perhaps it is better not. I have had so many nice letters from
people wishing me good luck that I feel all the more sorry I am
going ! " Finally, on August 31, there came the cry : " I am
frightfully sad at going ! It is awful ! "

After a last dinner with Henry Ainley and Charles La Trobe,
he was seen off at the station the next morning by several friends,
including Edwin Virgo, leader of the orchestra at the Haymarket,
where *The Dover Road* was then in the middle of its long run. At
2 p.m. on September 1 he was on board the *Empress of Britain* at
Liverpool, and trying hard to be " cheerful " : " Here I am !
My cabin is delightful ; lots of room."

During the voyage Norman wrote a few pages to Adine each
day, and he posted the resulting long letter when he reached
Quebec. Here are some extracts :

September 3, 1922.—. . . My cabin is comfortable—and my little bed soft,
but a bit small. The service is excellent, & the food, of which there is a vast
amount, excellent—with all kinds of extra turns between meals, like soup

at 11 a.m., tea at 4, & sandwiches are brought you before you go to bed. I ought to get quite fat. The ship is very well run, & there is *one* thing about the sea—it is so *clean*, & dust is unknown on board. I am lucky in having at my table three speechless old things. I do not utter either. I do not know what I should do if I was at a table with an American " party." They make nearly as much noise as the French ! There is not much deck room but I walk round and round until I have done a mile. Of course it is all painfully dull, & boresome to a degree, & there is nobody to talk to. It has gradually been getting rougher. . . . The boat is pitching now—if it *rolls* I know I shall be ill ! It is very cold. We are taking the extreme northern route, which is the quickest.

My day consists of getting up late. This is quite difficult, as we put the clock *back* every night, 40 minutes !—a long dressing & bath, then a long breakfast, then a short walk—lunch comes, & after that I go to sleep. I do a little scoring, dress for dinner, & go to bed at 10.30. . . .

September 4.—. . . A very rough night. The ship pitched & tossed to such an extent that it was impossible to sleep much. Feeling very dizzy from the noise & swinging about in my bath, I went back to bed & break-fasted there—only got up for lunch. I certainly *ought* to be seasick & cannot imagine why I am not. To-day the weather is bright, blue sky & very cold. . . .

The passengers consist of a vast majority of Americans—lots of this [*a drawing of a pair of horn-rimmed spectacles*]—quite good-looking women, in deck chairs, rows of them looking like a lot of old owls ! I get very bored with it all & I shall never take a sea voyage for pleasure. There is " music " at all the meals—& there is not a room where you can escape from the back-chat of the multitude. Without a cabin to oneself it would be " Oh God, oh Montreal ! " . . .

September 5.—What a change to-day !—a very quiet night & a lovely morning, mild & soft. The sea looks wonderful. We passed a large iceberg—a beautiful picture in the sun. The afternoon of yesterday was really tiresome —the cold & the continual motion all day long, & worse at night, of the boat, got well on my nerves. It was so rough that I could not do any scoring without making blots on the paper. . . . A lot of people have been seasick. Why I have escaped I cannot imagine ! Having exhausted the three books I brought, I am now reading Conrad's *Victory* again. It was the only thing not " out " in the ship's library worth while. Yesterday an American lady asked me if I was a " minister " ! So far I have remained incognito ! . . . My steward looks after me like a pet dog & brings me my breakfast in bed. . . .

September 6. — . . . That beautiful morning yesterday soon became clouded & dull again, & at nine o'clock at the mouth of the straits, off Belle Isle, we stopped dead. There was a heavy fog & as the straits are narrow they took no risks, as there were icebergs about. We remained motionless—quite motionless, as it was very calm, until 5.15 this morning, when the fog lifted. So we shall not get into the river to-day. We passed the wreck of the *Rayleigh* this morning & also nearly ran over a whale. . . . Last night there was a concert—which I did not attend. " Victory " is really fine. . . .

September 7.—In the St. Lawrence River—and still over one hundred miles to go before we reach Quebec. We are passing up this huge river near the south side, so one can see the hills & villages quite well. The other side is only a vague line, it is so far away. The customs officials have come on board—& there is an awful scrimmage going on on one of the decks.

Americans have to declare the value of every new thing they have bought, so you can imagine the talk that goes on. I shall not go down until late in the day, when the officials will be tired & glad to finish quickly ! . . .

" Passport, customs and red tape galore " made it impossible for Norman to see much of Quebec, and he had a hot and jolting journey to Montreal, where Avery Robinson was waiting for him on the platform. On September 9 they took the night train from Montreal, and after twelve hours reached North Bay, on Lake Nipissing. They changed trains and travelled fifty miles due south to Burks Falls. Then came a drive by car of about sixteen miles :

over what is called a road in Canada. You can have no idea of the jolting & shaking [wrote Norman]. It is just a forest track—over boulders, down into ruts, over old tree stumps. We should hardly call it a good climbing path ! It was all very fresh & quite an adventure. The country is very wild—mostly virgin woods with sometimes a cutting & a farm.

He was delighted with Avery Robinson's log house :

with a verandah all round—very wide—& partly closed in with sliding windows that can be open, with a lovely view down the lake. The lake is surrounded by low hills covered with woods, mostly pine & maple. . . . The country is not unlike the Black Forest in a way, but wilder, & the trees more varied—& of course there are all kinds of interesting game, porcupine, beavers, & a bear is said to be visiting the neighbourhood.

The next fortnight passed swiftly in a hospitable house which was " so homelike " that Norman could " hardly realise I am 3000 miles away." There were trips on the lake in a motor-boat and several excursions like one he mentioned :

A splendid tramp & shoot in glorious hot weather. The colouring gets more rich every day, & the maples are every shade from deep orange to crimson. The effect of hills round the lakes covered with maples & firs, in a red setting sun, is really wonderful.

Some work was done, too, and Norman completed the job of scoring which he had tackled under such difficulties on board the *Empress of Britain*. This music was for *Stigmata*, by John Rutherford (author of *The Breed of the Treshams*). *Stigmata* was often postponed, but Phyllis Neilson-Terry eventually played in it on a provincial tour in 1924. The end of Norman's score is dated " Forest Nook, September 26, 1922."

On the same day Norman left Forest Nook, having much enjoyed his stay, and took the train to Toronto, going on the next morning to Buffalo, Batavia, and Wyoming, where he spent two days with Avery Robinson's parents and his aunt, Mrs. Ward.

They motored him to Niagara Falls, about eighty miles each way.

> I cannot describe the Falls [wrote Norman]. It is quite true, they are one of the wonders of the world, and no mistake about it. It was a glorious day, & the spray & sun made two wonderful rainbows over the falls. It was most impressive, & moving.

On September 30, Mrs. Ward took him to the railway at Rochester, and at 10 p.m. that night he arrived in New York. A room had been reserved for him at the Hotel Woodstock in 43rd Street, which was conveniently near the Belasco Theatre in 44th Street, where they were to rehearse *The Merchant of Venice*.

David Belasco, then nearing seventy (he died in 1931), was a Jewish-American actor-manager-producer and dramatist who, as *The Times* said in his obituary notice, " in his time, and according to his lights, played a great part in the advancement of the theatre in America." In appearance, with his dark clothes, silvery hair and ascetic countenance, he looked like " a kindly old curé." " The play of his open features," said *The Times*, " was as diversified as his nature, which ranged from playfulness and tenderness to coldness or pugnacity. He could be kind or adamant, sympathetic or obtuse. His weaknesses, such as a craving for admiration, were balanced by fine judgment in affairs and a well-applied knowledge of humanity." Belasco wrote or collaborated in a great number of plays ; he discovered Mary Pickford ; he built the Stuyvesant Theatre and owned and managed the Belasco Theatre and many other theatres ; and in the course of all these activities he had amassed a fortune.

Though he did not often concern himself with Shakespeare, this production of *The Merchant of Venice* was one of Belasco's enthusiasms and he had spared no trouble or expense to make it a success. The cast he had collected included Philip Merivale as Bassanio, Mary Servoss as Portia, Mary Ellis (since seen in many musical comedies in England) as Nerissa, and David Warfield, one of the greatest attractions of the American stage, as Shylock. It was the last big part that Warfield played before his retirement.

For the next two months Norman worked at close quarters with these two well-known American theatrical figures, Belasco and Warfield. On October 5 he wrote to Adine :

> Everything so far going well — & much enthusiasm about the music. Old Belasco is a dear old soul, & I get on with him all right. Nothing could

be kinder than they all are, and everything is done to make things easy and comfortable. The Belasco Theatre is a world in itself—B's rooms, studio, etc., are at the top, & are very comfortable & picturesque. He has some beautiful things. I usually lunch with him & Warfield in his private dining-room, the old man dressed in silk pyjamas & a dressing-gown. . . .

On October 6 Norman wrote :

. . . My time has mostly been taken up by hearing singers, etc. The Jewish choir is going to be quite good, but the man who they engaged to play the jester,[1] before I came, is a musical idiot, & I spend hours trying to teach him those two simple songs ! I have the first rehearsal actually with the play on Monday. Then " Mr. B " will start his experimenting I expect, & much patience & endurance will be required. This week he managed to scald his leg with boiling coffee, which brought everything to a standstill !— However, last night he took us all out to see a variety show. It is his custom to go to the theatre with all his staff on Friday evenings & see some show ! . . . From Monday onwards he feeds the whole company, as he likes to have everybody on the premises all the time.

. . . The conductor is a Hungarian, a nice fellow, & seems to be an excellent musician. I am glad I have plenty to do, as I feel very homesick at odd moments. When the first impression has worn off, this town gets on one's nerves. Its ugliness is terrific.

A week later Norman reported :

We are very busy—in the theatre from 10 to 7 every day. It is going well but rather slowly. Belasco seems very pleased with all my effects, etc. We are keeping it all very simple & I think the result will be good. I have seen a good deal of Grimwood, such a nice " old " Bensonian, who plays with us in the play.[2] He took me to dine at an Italian place, where we got sparkling Italian wine. Last night I took him to dine at another Italian place where we had such good cheap food, & red wine in tea cups. Afterwards we went to see *The Faithful Heart*. Better done than in London— Tom Nesbitt, who played here in *Mary Rose*, excellent. We had supper with him at his flat after the play. I saw Alexandra Carlisle. She is playing in an excellent play called *Fool's Errant*. She has asked me to dine with them next week. I fear that will not be possible if Belasco rehearses at night, which he threatens to do. The vitality of the old man is wonderful. He rushes about the stage all day, shouting and *making* them act ! . . .

But despite Belasco's energy, progress was not entirely satisfactory, and on October 18 misgivings began to assert themselves :

It is all going very slowly—the old man is dreadfully longwinded ! . . . As far as the music is concerned the rehearsals have not been much use yet. Belasco keeps everybody in the theatre, if they are wanted or not ! He certainly seems able to produce women, but there it stops. If he is able to make anything of the Portia he will indeed be a marvel. He loves to show off,

---

[1] Belasco introduced this character. In the same way the small part of the " First Fairy " became an important ingredient in Reinhardt's *Midsummer Night's Dream*. Belasco also made other debatable alterations.

[2] Herbert Grimwood, who played the Prince of Morocco.

& preaches at the company by the hour, but in spite of that one cannot help liking him, although he pumps everybody for ideas which come out as his own afterwards. The money that has been spent is amazing. One of Portia's dresses from Paris cost £1200 (pounds !). . . .

Four days later, all was again

Going very well, & the old man, Belasco, wept to-day after the song " Tell me where is fancy bred " with its *pp* vocal accompaniment. He says he will hate to see me go away ! I have put in some very effective moments that grew at rehearsal. . . .

The long hours of rehearsal did not give Norman many opportunities of seeing New York life, but he did go one night " to a huge ' movie house ' with a splendid orchestra of about seventy (!)," and he was able to visit two clubs which had elected him to honorary membership : the Players, with its beautiful old Georgian house, and the Harvard Club, where he wrote his letter in a replica of a Cambridge hall. But on the whole, though he thought it " a curious mixture," he failed to find " anything distinctive in New York."

Norman's respect for Belasco as a producer gradually increased, but he hated to see his extravagance and waste :

(*October 25*).—. . . They say he will have spent £50,000 on the production before it gets to New York. This is, I think, an absurd thing to do, & money is wasted in a wicked way. He, Belasco, is a wonderful producer—& when I tell you he has to teach everything to Shylock & Portia, as well as to a host of small parts, you can imagine what he has undertaken. The only people who know their jobs are the English actors. . . .

(*November 2*).—We had stage orchestra [1] yesterday & everybody is in raptures at the music. It *is* certainly effective. I have a very good soprano to sing " Tell me where is fancy bred " with accompaniment of men's voices, harp, & strings. . . . I find the conductor most helpful & he is such a nice little man, & I do not let Belasco bully him, which he much appreciates. The scenery is rather a disappointment, but the electrician is a genius & will probably do the trick. The dresses also, in spite of the wonderful stuffs, rather lack imagination, & are just copies of the real thing—like the scenery. You know my views on theatre, & all art—I hate photos ! . . .

(*November 3*).—" I am evidently popular, as I have received a consignment of pre-war whisky from Belasco ! He is a quaint old bird, with his young lady friends, & his *vitality*. He is an extraordinary mixture of humbug and real talent. . . .

The praise of the music was justified, for this was perhaps the most successful of Norman's Shakespearean ventures. As Mr. Ernest Irving has said, the music, somehow or other, imparted a genuine Venetian atmosphere to the play. Endless trouble had

---

[1] Some of the music in this production was played by a small orchestra off-stage.

been taken, long in advance, in working out a musical scheme, as the following random quotations from the typed " music plot " show :

Prelude to Second Act plays to Curtain up, 3 minutes and 50 seconds :
From Curtain up to Enter Tubal, about 17 seconds :
From Enter Tubal to Enter Chus, about 37 seconds :
From Enter Chus to Enter Launcelot Gobbo, about 15 seconds :
From Enter Launcelot Gobbo to the end of the number, about 10 seconds. . . .

And later :

As written by Mr. O'Neill, Prelude to Fourth Act plays 5 minutes and 25 seconds. And it goes right into Prince of Morocco music, which plays for 2 minutes and 23 seconds. . . . At cue " thus losers part " repeat last 9 bars of Prelude. Portia speaks upon cue of a certain note in the Morocco music, " A gentle riddance." Upon Portia's words " his complexion choose me so," hunting horns are heard off, etc. etc.

On Sunday, November 5, the Belasco company left New York and travelled a hundred miles southwards to Wilmington, Delaware ; and later in the same day Norman rehearsed the full orchestra of twenty-nine players for the first time. They stayed at the Hotel du Pont, " a fine hotel & the theatre is in the same building. Belasco ' entertains ' the whole company, 65 people, at lunch and dinner." The intention was to give the first performance at Wilmington on November 10, but they had to go on another fifty miles, to Baltimore, without having done so. Norman wrote in the train to Baltimore on the following Sunday :

We did not produce at Wilmington. The scenery held us up, so we had these endless rehearsals all the week, some lasting 36 hours ! I have never seen anything like the waste of time & money. When I tell you, you will say I am exaggerating. £50,000 will not cover it—& the scenery is rotten. But the play will be well done—& the dresses, the English actors, & the music will probably do the trick ! . . .

Norman found Baltimore a relief after New York, and was pleased to see " some streets of charming Georgian houses, and a sort of smart street strangely like Bond Street." He stayed at the old-fashioned Stafford Hotel with its negro staff. A letter of November 15 describes the final dress rehearsal and eventual first performance of *The Merchant of Venice* at Ford's Opera House, Baltimore :

. . . On Monday morning we had a rehearsal with the local orchestra, which was excellent. And as our own 15 men now know it perfectly I was quite delighted with the result. Dress rehearsal Monday night—& then the trouble began ! All on account of the scenery, which is so elaborate & unpractical that they cannot handle it. The rehearsal dragged on until 5.30 a.m.

& we did not do the last Act in which there is so much music. Everybody was dead beat—people asleep on the floor all over the place, & everything going wrong, including the music, singing, etc. It was pitiful to see old Belasco quite broken up, all the fire gone out of him, as he gradually realised, what he had been told by the staff but would not listen to, that Gros, a French artist who has designed for him for 30 years, had let him down. We all feel so sorry for him.

After we had all gone home to bed Belasco stayed on in the theatre, & *woke* up, & there was an unholy row. The poor jaded staff & an army of workmen then set to work to alter the scenes so that they could be staged by last night. And they certainly worked wonders, & at the show last night they got through without excessive waits. In fact, what with good playing, good lighting, & the music, I think it was a fine first performance. The music was beautifully done & the audience was quiet during the preludes & applauded them, and the music evidently made an impression. The conductor was splendid & worked all the stage music effects beautifully. After that awful rehearsal there was no glamour or excitement for me of a first night—only anxiety !

The old man was pleased, and awfully nice to me. We all went out to supper with him—but without any stimulant this jaded company was not very exciting.

In New York Norman had had grave doubts about Warfield's Shylock. " If Warfield is not a success it will be a fiasco," he had declared ; " at present he is nothing." But in the end Warfield did not let them down ; and Norman wrote from Baltimore :

Warfield was very fine, & will be finer. He has a great personality—perhaps a little too modest & sympathetic for Shylock. Belasco says we " now start real work," so I suppose we shall rehearse every day.

. . . I hear Belasco has put his whole spare capital into this production—& more than half of it (£20,000) has been wasted. It cost a quarter of a million dollars ! The orchestra bill was 2000 dollars last week for rehearsal—& I could have done it with 6 hours rehearsals if I had had my way. It is awful to see this waste going on. . . .

From Baltimore Norman went over for a day to Washington, and on the next Sunday he travelled nearly two hundred miles with the company to Pittsburg, an interesting journey through beautiful mountain country. In Pittsburg he found :

A nice theatre, but an awful town. It is in a hole, with hills round it, so the smoke from thousands of factories never gets away & it is as dirty as Sheffield. A huge hotel—very hot—if you have the window open you are covered with dirt, & if you have it shut you are roasted. . . .

The Pittsburg audience was cold and the company were therefore depressed, but the local orchestral players were excellent and with Belasco's fifteen gave a fine performance of the music. The next Sunday they went on to Cleveland, Ohio, on Lake

XII.—LOSELY FARM, NEAR EWHURST

XIII.—4 PEMBROKE VILLAS

Erie. There Norman left them, returning to New York to sail for England in the *Olympic* on December 2. The unexpected delays, and the protracted tour, made it impossible for him to stay for the first performance in New York.

The play was well received when it was seen at the Lyceum Theatre, New York, on December 31, and its run of ninety-two consecutive performances was a record for *The Merchant of Venice* in America. During his stay Norman had had several negotiations with New York music publishers. He had hoped that a piano version and a suite for orchestra from the *Merchant of Venice* music would be published ; but he could not accept the offered terms, and in the end three songs only were published by the H. W. Gray Company : " Tell me where is Fancy bred," and " It was a Lover and his Lass," and the part-song " Come away Death "—the two last introduced by Belasco from *As You Like It* and *Twelfth Night*.

Norman had much enjoyed the trip and the experience of meeting Belasco and Warfield, but he was very glad to get back to England. He was tired of the " everlasting *Merchant* talk," and said " One even gets sick of praise ! "

CHAPTER XIII

DEMAND AND SUPPLY

THE studio in which Norman's music was written stood in the garden of 4 Pembroke Villas, away from the house. It was a square building with a corrugated iron roof (under which starlings nested), and, having been originally built for an artist, it had a large north window. In Norman's time the walls of dark brown natural pine were hung with old German engravings, a few water-colours, and a large unfinished oil-painting by G. B. O'Neill. Photographs of Norman's boyhood home, Willesley, sketches by his father, and caricatures by fellow-members of the Savage Club were propped up on shelves. An old copper warming-pan and a native drum hung upon the wall ; a spear with a red-velvet handle stood in a corner. There was a broken flute in the beautiful Chippendale bookcase, beside many books of poetry, old and new, the latter given him by hopeful authors who hoped he might set one of their poems to music.

A large square table in front of the window was covered with masses of manuscript, bills and receipts under paper weights, and a silver tray full of sealing wax, pins, nibs, rubbers, broken pen-knives and clips. The grand piano, kept out of tune because Norman preferred it so, was similarly covered with manuscript and printed music, and there was still more music in a Brittany bed which had been converted into a cupboard.

The studio was heated by a stove which, assisted by the smoke from Norman's pipe, made it snug in winter. It was remote from the house and domestic worries. Those who knew it best felt that the thirty years of music-making in that room gave it an atmosphere of its own—the same feeling of something apart from this life which permeates Norman's music and takes the hearer away from the everyday world.

For several years from 1923 onwards the studio was a very busy place. The demand for Norman's music was constant. Indeed, at one time it seemed almost inevitable that a theatre programme should contain the words " Incidental Music composed by Norman O'Neill." It may have been in a way a sort of supremely successful musical journalism ; but, if so, it was journalism of the highest class. " As a musician of the theatre it is a question if we have ever produced a better man than Norman

O'Neill," wrote Sir Dan Godfrey, who felt that Norman had the best sense of the theatre of any British musician since Hamilton Clarke.

Probably the first time Norman's music was heard after his return from America was at the opening on January 1, 1923, of the short-lived Play-box Theatre, South Kensington, when the music was for a children's play by Miles Malleson. Norman wrote three songs (two were published) for Ernest Temple Thurston's *A Roof and Four Walls*, produced at the Apollo Theatre in the same month, and his close friendship with the author led him to compose the delightful song-cycle based on five poems about birds in a collection by Temple Thurston, published later in the year. The cuckoo was the first of the birds :

> Cuckoo, I can hear love's token,
> Cuckoo, your sweet note is broken.
> You have lost your April touch—
> Cuckoo—must you love so much ?

and the other songs were dedicated to the wren, the wagtail, the night-jar, and lastly the woodpecker :

> Hammer—hammer—hammer
> On the hard oak tree—
> What a mighty blacksmith
> You must be ! . . .

Norman had a bad attack of phlebitis in 1923 and was compelled to stay in bed for three weeks. It was painful, but he was wonderfully cheerful and managed to write an " Irish Jig " for Leslie Bridgewater's Quintet. He also composed for A. A. Milne's *Success* at the Haymarket in June, 1923, and when *Success* refused to live up to its name, he wrote some excellent music, published by Cramer, for a happy revival of *The Prisoner of Zenda*, with Robert Loraine and Fay Compton, which followed it. His next important work was done for Archibald de Bear's charming revue, *The Punch Bowl*, which was enthusiastically received when it opened at the Duke of York's on May 21, 1924. The revue was in three parts, and as *The Times* said the next morning :

The middle section is the most ambitious and by far the most pleasing. It sets out to show us the familiar " Punch and Judy show " as it might be if brought up to date, and . . . we are given a " Punch and Judy " ballet, to music by Mr. Norman O'Neill, which is wholly delightful. . . . Mr. O'Neill's music has a great share in the success of this ballet, and the whole is a delight to the eye, to the ear, and also to the intelligence.

The Punch Bowl ran for well over a year, and Mr. de Bear continued his association with Norman in a worthy successor, *R.S.V.P.*, which was produced at the Vaudeville in February 1926. The same plan was followed of having a middle section devoted to ballet, this time an " Alice in Wonderland " ballet by Clifford Pember, in which an old booklover conjured Alice from his bookshelf followed by all the inhabitants of Wonderland. Here Norman used many well-known melodies. The chief theme of the work was an inversion of the tune " Alice, where art thou " ; the Dormouse fell asleep to " Three Blind Mice," the gardeners painted the white rose trees to " My love is like a red, red rose " ; and the Queen's dance with Alice was nearly " You should see me dance the polka." When the Queen ordered the executions she did so to a theme suggesting " Off with his head," and this changed to a *valse lente* (the Alice theme, correctly played) during which the Gryphon capered " Roger de Coverley." Of course the Lobsters had their quadrille.

" Mr. O'Neill gives us ideal music for ' Alice in Wonderland,' " said *The Times*. " Miss Mimi Crawford gives us the ideal Alice." So thought Norman's daughter, when she was taken behind the scenes at a matinée and had tea with Mimi Crawford in her stage costume. Of his " very pleasant association with Norman O'Neill," Mr. Archie de Bear writes :

I most clearly remember his constant helpfulness in the rehearsals of his charming music for my " Punch and Judy " and " Alice " ballets, and the cheerful effect on these rehearsals of his genial personality. His music contributed very largely indeed to the success of the shows concerned— just as his presence was in itself a considerable part of the show in those rare occasions, like first nights, when he conducted in person. I have had by me for a long time a film adaptation I prepared of " Punch and Judy up to date." It includes a sequence representing the ballet, and in it I suggested that the commanding and picturesque figure of the composer, Norman O'Neill, would be of great value in the actual picture. Unfortunately, I could find no market for the film, and it still remains unproduced.

The music for both ballets was published, and has been a good deal played. But this account of Norman's successful incursion into revue—not quite complete, for he also composed for the *Potiniere Revue* at the Little in October, 1926—has carried us past several other interesting productions with which he was concerned.

The first of these was a revival, at the Haymarket, at Christmas 1924, of Barrie's *A Kiss for Cinderella*, with Norman McKinnel —not perhaps quite so elegant a *petit maître* as Gerald du Maurier—

making a capital figure of fun of the Policeman, and with Hilda Trevelyan in her original part as Cinderella, J. H. Roberts as Mr. Bodie and Lady Tree as the Queen. Norman was in his element here, and provided music for Barrie's amusing second act which deserves to be as permanently associated with this play as his other music is with *Mary Rose*.

Next came an equally successful revival, in April 1925, at the New Oxford Theatre, of Edward Knoblock's *Kismet*. The play had first been produced in 1911, with Oscar Asche and Lily Brayton, and had been revived with them in 1914. For the 1925 revival Sam Livesey took the part of Haji, Elissa Landi played Marsinah, and Benita Hume and Mary Clare were in smaller parts. James Agate said that the music showed " Mr. Norman O'Neill at his most Baghdacious " ; but in fact he did not attempt too much orientalism, and, as in Lord Dunsany's plays, was content to give a suggestion of the East in music that was as distinctive and delicate as any of his work. Three songs and three dances were published.

In May, 1925, Ashley Dukes's comedy, *The Man with a Load of Mischief*, began its long run at the Haymarket in the charming scene designed for it by Norman's friend, Aubrey Hammond, who was rapidly acquiring the same reputation in the theatre for scenery as Norman had already acquired for music. Norman composed two songs, published by Cramer, and two preludes for *The Man with a Load of Mischief*. Mr. Ashley Dukes writes : " He invited me to listen carefully to his music at the dress rehearsal of the play, or rather to the overture he had arranged and composed—I think the arrangement must have owed something to Dr. Arne—and said this was the only opportunity I should ever have of hearing it. He did not mean luckily that the play would only run one night, but that people in the audience never stop talking until the curtain rises. . . ."

The only negative note in this year of good fortune was sounded by Monckton Hoffe's *Cristilinda*, produced at the Garrick in October 1925, with Isobel Elsom and Allan Aynesworth. *Cristilinda* began well, but proved over-sentimental, and, moreover, was not well cast. James Agate concluded his notice :

It would be very interesting to discover how this piece would play with Cristilinda acted by some child-actress of genius . . . and the circus-master given by an actor with a sense of buffoonery who did not remind one of the late Mr. Gladstone perorating under one of Hawarden's oaks. In these conditions it might be worthy of Mr. Norman O'Neill's delightful incidental music.

In 1926 Boosey published *Echoes of Erin*, a collection of twelve famous old Irish songs for which Norman had arranged the music. " It is not for me to appraise the technicalities of music," wrote Dr. Douglas Hyde, later President of Eire, in a preface, " but many of us will welcome to the ranks of folk-song arrangers such a musician as Norman O'Neill." The book was dedicated to Norman's old teacher, Sir Arthur Somervell.

These were the years in which the B.B.C. at Savoy Hill first established, and then rapidly developed, its musical activities. Adine, who had served as President of the Society of Women Musicians from 1921 to 1923, began to play for the B.B.C. in the summer of 1924, when she broadcast three new piano pieces by Gerard Williams. Pianists in those days were not on the whole keen to play without an audience in the room with them ; but Adine had always been shy of an audience, and she welcomed the idea. Thereafter, she broadcast very frequently. She often took part in the " Foundations of Music " series, playing all the Mozart sonatas in two consecutive weeks, and another time she played the Haydn sonatas ; she also gave a week of seventeenth- and eighteenth-century music (of which two evenings were devoted to Scarlatti), and a week of modern French music.

The wireless now carried her playing into the homes of distant friends. " We have a radio here on trial and we hear you playing Mozart every evening," wrote Mrs. Delius from Grez-sur-Loing in May 1926. " You certainly play it beautifully. What an extraordinary invention!" And the next year she said: "We listened to your playing last night. . . . Fred liked the Scarlatti best. We both admired your pearly technique."

Another staunch admirer of Adine's playing was Gustav Holst, who dedicated to her his first important piano piece, a toccata based on the Northumbrian pipe tune " Newburn Lads," which he composed in the summer of 1924. " For many years I have tried to write a piano piece for Mrs. O'Neill," he wrote to Dr. W. Gillies Whittaker, " and this summer I have at last succeeded. And I finished it just in time to send it with an appropriate dedication to her on her silver wedding." He also composed a little piece for Yvonne. Holst waited eagerly for Adine's broadcasts, especially enjoying her playing of Scarlatti. In 1932 he wrote to her from St. Paul's Girls' School :

Amongst all that you have done for me the two things I am most grateful for are, firstly, introducing me to Scarlatti and then bringing me here. And it is high time I had more of the former. . . .

One of the last letters Holst wrote to anyone was written to Adine after he had heard her play on the wireless :

BEAUFORT HOUSE, EALING, W. 5,
May 20. 8 p.m. [1934].

DEAR ADINE,—The great treat is just over and so I write at once to thank you very very much for it.

But I hope I shall never have to go so long without hearing you—it must be nearly a year which is ridiculous. One thing that will help to bring us together soon is that my operation is fixed for next Wednesday. It is a great relief after all this waiting.

Nora and Vally [1] will keep you and the rest of St. Paul's posted up with the latest news.

Again, many thanks. And love,—Yrs Gratefully,

GUSTAV.

Although the operation was successful, the heart proved unequal to the strain and Holst died on May 25.

Norman at first was far from enthusiastic about the wireless. He did not march briskly in the ranks of scientific progress, for he kept taking longing glances over his shoulder at the world of his youth. " A wonderful invention ! " he would say sarcastically, when the atmospherics spoiled a song or when a car in which he was driving broke down at a critical moment. But with Adine's example before him, he soon came to appreciate the merits, as well as the uses, of broadcasting, and from January 1925 his name appeared regularly, two or three times each year, as composer or conductor for B.B.C. programmes. Thus he composed music for the wireless version of Reginald Berkeley's *The White Château*, given on November 11, 1925. He also several times conducted programmes of his own compositions for the B.B.C. ; and *Mary Rose, Kismet, The Pretenders,* and a number of lighter productions were broadcast with his music.

Adine always played under her married name as Mrs. Norman O'Neill, but journalists and others sometimes callously chopped the " s " off " Mrs." and made Norman a solo pianist as well as a composer and conductor. In 1910 a musical paper described " Norman O'Neill's recent appearance before the Oxford Ladies' Musical Society," playing Schumann, Scarlatti, and Chopin, and went on to say that there was " no more popular musician in London " than the composer of the music for *The Blue Bird*. A sigh from Adine and Norman's vigorous laugh can be heard at this point. And readers of Rose Macaulay's *Crewe Train*, at least in the Penguin edition, are told that " Arnold put on a pair

[1] Miss Nora Day and Miss Vally Lasker, music teachers at St. Paul's Girls' School.

of earphones, and prepared to listen to Mozart's Sonata in D Major, interpreted by Mr. Norman O'Neill."

As a matter of fact, Norman himself was an excellent pianist, though not of course a solo performer. He once promised Julian Clifford, Senior, that he would play the piano part in a composition for piano and orchestra at Harrogate ; all went well at rehearsal, but at the last minute, perhaps, his courage failed, and he and Clifford changed places—Norman conducting and Clifford playing. However, he certainly accompanied Henry Ainley at Harrogate in Richard Strauss's melodramatic recitation," Enoch Arden."

Adine got her own back when the musical comedy, *Rose Marie*, was produced in Paris. Louis Aubert, the composer and critic, wrote Norman a letter of congratulation, and declared in a French paper that he had composed the music for *Rose Marie*. Norman had to write, rather wistfully, to Aubert to explain that *Rose Marie*, the musical comedy, and *Mary Rose*, by J. M. Barrie, were very different things.

CHAPTER XIV

LOSELY

. . . O, the green fields of Surrey, the sweet fields of Surrey,
The dear fields of Surrey, I'll love till I die.
                                        WILLIAM C. BENNETT.

SINCE 1922 Norman and Adine had been looking for a country
cottage, where they could now and then rest from the labours
of their London life ; and in 1924 Norman heard that a lovely
old house was for sale in a part of Surrey he had been fond of
since boyhood. It was an Elizabethan farmhouse called Losely,
delightfully situated on rising ground near Ewhurst, close to
Pitch Hill and Holmbury Hill. Norman went down to see it,
and fell in love with it at once. Yet he returned home quite
depressed ; he felt, after seeing Losely, that nothing else could
possibly satisfy him, but at the same time he knew he could not
afford to buy it.

Adine then went down to the house, and although she noticed
with dismay such details as the distance from Ewhurst village and
Ockley station (they had no car), and the absence of electricity
and gas, she also fell completely in love with the beauty of the
place. Eventually she decided to ask her mother if she could
possibly help them to buy it. Madame Philippi was most
sympathetic, and, with her assistance and that of a good friend
of Norman, Losely became theirs.

Losely Farm is said to have been at one time a hunting-box
on the then large estates of the More family of Loseley, near
Guildford, and to have derived its name from this association.
Ghosts are included among the amenities. There is a tradition
that the house is haunted by Drake and Raleigh, who are supposed to sit by the open fireplace in the dining-room on Christmas
Eve. The O'Neills were not in a position to confirm the legend,
as they never spent Christmas at Losely, but it is true that
visitors in the spare-room sometimes heard footsteps in the
early morning and a mysterious rat-tat at the door, and would
blithely get up and dress, thinking it was time for breakfast.
Norman scorned spiritualism, but, as befitted the composer
of the *Mary Rose* music, he took ghosts and fairies perfectly
seriously, and indeed used to tell various stories of his own
experiences.

A long drive led to the house, which was quite hidden from the main road. In front of it was a terrace overlooking a lily pond, which on the far side was level with the lawn. From the terrace there was a lovely view (Temple Thurston painted it) of meadows and woods, with Pitch Hill to the right in the middle distance. The farmhouse was long and narrow, and had at one time been divided into two cottages ; it had a roof of Horsham slabs. At the back, on the slope of a little hill, was a kitchen garden, and there were also a small orchard, a stable and a barn.

Inside, the ceiling of one room had been taken down, so as to make a room the height of the house. This was the main sitting-room, and there was an old pump in it. The dining-room, like the rest of Losely, had many old oak beams, some with the ships' initials and marks of the Elizabethan period.

One of the first things Norman did at Losely was to buy a white donkey and a donkey-cart with yellow wheels. " Neddy " had an erratic nature, but she was useful for what she could produce for Norman's flower beds, which was perhaps the chief reason for buying her. On the day of her arrival Norman shut her up in the stable, but Yvonne opened the door to have a look at her, and out flew " Neddy," trotting like the wind down the drive and out into the main road. She was making for her old home, the Bull's Head, at Ewhurst. Norman tore after her—cursing, because to run hurt his bad leg—and Yvonne dashed across a field to try and intercept. But they were too late, and had to go all the way to the Bull's Head, and then pull her home again.

After this, Norman became rather sceptical about the possibilities of " Neddy." His distrust increased when he discovered that she invariably went downhill sideways. Eventually " Neddy," coming down Holmbury Hill, upset the cart, and with it Norman O'Neill, bad leg and all. He did not go in the donkey-cart again ; instead, a small blue Singer was purchased. It had a folding hood, and mica windows, which were soon broken. Neither Norman nor Adine could drive the Singer, any more than they could manage the donkey, but their friend Freda Heymann stayed a whole summer at Losely to drive it for them and fetched many week-end visitors from Ockley station. Aubrey Hammond, whom his friends described as "the largest artist in captivity," provided the severest test for the Singer. On that trip no other passenger was allowed.

Losely gave Norman perfect scope for his talent in rearing an old-world garden, and he worked wonders in his flower-beds.

He and Adine kept open house ; the meals were frequent and large. Yet, like Robert Bloomfield, he might have cried :

> Sweet health, I seek thee ! hither bring
> Thy balm that softens human ills ;
> Come, on the long-drawn clouds that fling
> Their shadows o'er the Surrey Hills. . . .

And here Losely failed him, for the house was built on clay soil, which made his leg ache terribly, and he never felt really well there.

After his attack of phlebitis in 1923, Norman went yearly to Bagnoles-de-l'Orne to take a cure for his varicose veins. The waters there gave him the only real relief he ever experienced, and after the cure he could always count on six months of tolerable health. He hated a lot of luggage, and much to Adine's dismay used to leave for Bagnoles with only a small suitcase, containing pyjamas, two shirts, a few collars, socks, etc. When he got there he did a little washing each day, and hung his collars, socks and shirt outside the window to dry. He wrote the following letter to his daughter from Bagnoles, after she had been made head girl of her school :

Sunday.

DARLING YVONNE,—Many thanks for your nice long letter & report, which I suppose will cost me something ! Why is it called a Head Girl— is it a girl with a Head, or a head with a girl ? Why did they choose you ? I am sorry your passages are not good on the violin, & that your finger work on the 'cello is careless.[1] This must be attended to. It is quite appropriate that your religious knowledge should be good in parts, for was not the curate's egg ? No, joking apart, you've evidently got to put your back into it next term !

I'm three-quarters through this cure now, I'm glad to say. You would be amused at the costumes people wear in the mornings going to the baths. In the bus are the following :

(1) Gent fully dressed, overcoat, tie, pin, black hat, striped trousers, boots, walking-stick, racing-glasses. Might be going to Epsom.
(2) Soldier. Full uniform, sword, spurs, huge cloak, etc.
(3) Smart young thing in pyjamas. Rouge, perfume, etc.
(4) Old lady in heavy dressing-gown, huge slippers, six shawls.
(5) Old man. Beret, two overcoats, six waistcoats.
(6) Myself in flannel trousers & overcoat.

Very comic. Of course they take so long undressing & dressing that I have to wait ages in the bus coming out of the baths until they are ready ! Weather has been awful—yesterday & to-day are the first fine days we have had. I'm sending a book to you & to Mother. Thank her for her letter. Love to you both,

FATHER.

---

[1] An elaborate joke, for Yvonne learned neither of these instruments.

At the bottom of the page appeared the words " Turn over,"
and the other side was headed, " To Adine & Yvonne " :

> *A*ll letters I've received, & some
> *L*ong time they seem to take to come.
> *L*ong letters, too, so many thanks—
> *L*eave here on Sat for Lo-ing's banks.[1]
> *O*nly one week more of this dull curing
> *V*eins varicose. Its more than boring.
> *E*ach day, & hour, I count with care !
> *T*o-day the sun is bright, the weather rare,
> *O*nly it will not last they all declare.
> *Y*et, spite of rain, & cold, my legs are bare !
> *O*h yes, to walk again with you I'll learn,
> *U*p miles of hills, & down, when we return.
> *B*ut now unravel this, look carefully ;
> *O*nce down, not up, or horizontally—
> '*T*is very simple if you read *one* side
> *H*ow words can thus their inner meaning hide !
>
> *N*ow you'll know how to send, on provocation,
> *O*'n good Saint Val'tine's day, a declaration !
> *N*ow try & read aright my poor creation !

The expense of two houses made it necessary for the O'Neills
to let Losely from time to time, and a run of ill-success for Norman's stage productions increased the difficulty of keeping it. He
still poured out music as busily as ever. Several part-songs
and unison-songs, a suite for piano, and the " Festal Prelude "
and two Shakespearean sketches for orchestra were published in
the years 1925–28—the " Festal Prelude," dedicated to Basil
Cameron, being composed for the opening of the White Rock
Pavilion, Hastings, on April 6, 1927. At this opening concert
Norman not only conducted his Prelude but also a performance
by George Baker of the " La Belle Dame sans Merci." He often
took part in the concerts at Hastings, where Julius Harrison
later succeeded Cameron as director, and Harrogate, East-
bourne and Margate were among other seaside places where
he conducted his works. He had helped Dan Godfrey at Bourne-
mouth as early as 1901.

The first stage performance of Berkeley's *The White Château*
was given at Hampstead in March 1927, and the play went to
the St. Martin's Theatre the following month. Norman's music,
originally commissioned by the B.B.C., was now adapted for the
theatre, and he also agreed to provide music for a film version
of the play, though this was not proceeded with. Not all the
plays for which he composed music at this time are worth

[1] He was going to Grez-sur-Loing to stay with Delius. This was in August 1932.

recording, but at Christmas 1928 he enjoyed himself arranging carols and incidental music for the Haymarket production of *Mr. Pickwick*, by Cosmo Hamilton and Frank C. Reilly. Stage adaptations from Dickens are tricky things, but with Charles Laughton as Pickwick and Mary Clare as Mrs. Bardell, this was indeed, as *The Times* said, " a happy extravaganza . . . a rollicking, practical fantasy," and it deserved a longer run than it obtained. Herman Finck in his reminiscences has this story about the play :

> Unknown to O'Neill, some loud-speakers had been installed in the auditorium with a microphone in a room at the back of the stage, for amplifying effects. The distant coach horn from the approaching Pickwickian coach was also played in this room, but by some mistake the microphone was switched on when the horn cue came. The result was that an awful blast resounded in the theatre. Norman flew out of the orchestra and into the room where the horn player was, and told him in good round terms what he thought of him. Norman did not know that the microphone was carrying his vigorous language straight to the audience ! . . .

Norman wrote music to be played between the acts when Reginald Berkeley's *The Lady with the Lamp* was produced at the Garrick in January 1929. But two other productions of that year were less successful : A. A. Milne's graceful fable, *The Ivory Door*, did not strike deep enough ; and, despite Norman's " Baghdacious " dances and Edmund Dulac's scenery and dresses, *The Shadow of the East*, adapted by Mr. and Mrs. Vernon from the French, was not a second *Kismet*. He was happier writing music for a special performance at the Haymarket— in honour of Shakespeare's birthday anniversary in April 1929— of *Measure for Measure*, which he used to say was his favourite Shakespeare play. This careful production, with Jean Forbes Robertson as Isabella, merited a longer life. Norman's music was also used for two birthday performances of *Hamlet* at the Haymarket in 1930, when Henry Ainley headed an all-star cast including many of the best-known actors on the English stage, down to Ernest Thesiger as Osric and Cedric Hardwicke as the First Gravedigger. A command performance of this unique production was given before the King and Queen in May 1930, and it was revived for a month, with Godfrey Tearle as Hamlet, in the following year.

It is perhaps unnecessary to state that the longer the run of a play with his music, the more Norman stood to benefit financially. From one point of view, therefore, it was a drawback that the plays for which his incidental music was required were usually just those imaginative, intelligent pieces which carry with them the highest risk of failure. So long as he was working on the scripts of writers like Maeterlinck and Barrie, this risk, though not absent, was less actual ; but the supply of genius of this sort is limited, and in the late 1920's showed signs of running out. Though he had no lack of work, there were few plays for which he composed during the last years of his life about which he did not have qualms that were all too often justified ; and the progressive reduction, for the sake of economy, in the size of theatre orchestras gave him continual anxiety.

Only Shakespeare remained comparatively safe, and latterly Norman's thoughts were turning increasingly to Shakespeare, to the new prospects opened up by the cinema, and indeed to any quarter that promised a reasonable return, provided always that it did not involve him in " writing down " to a lower level. In 1930 he composed music for an effective one-act play by H. C. G. Stevens called *To Meet the King !* in which Sybil Thorndike played at the London Coliseum. Play and music were recorded for the gramophone, an ironic freak of fate, considering how much of Norman's best music has gone unrecorded.

It was the 1930 slump that finally made it necessary to sell Losely. Norman and Adine were sorry to give it up, but as a matter of fact, apart from not feeling well there, Norman had always found it hard to compose in the country. He used to say " Nature is so disturbing." Instead of concentrating on his work, he found himself listening to the birds or looking at the view. Nevertheless, one delightful, most alive and tuneful work was written there, a setting of Herbert Asquith's poem, " The Farmer and the Fairies," as a recitation with piano or orchestral accompaniment. The poem tells how miserly Farmer Jelf had the misfortune to offend the fairies, and how they spirited away his hoard of guineas :

> And every piece of gold took wing
> From hidden crannies in wall and stair
> And shimmered out on the midnight air,
> And the farmer galloped across the wold,
> To ride in chase of the flying gold.

> He never came back. On Tilbarrow hill
> They say that he is hunting still :
> By Shapcut Edge and Cranberry Moss,
> Down the slope by the Hangman's Cross,
> And up the brow near the Miller's Stone
> They have seen him gallop and heard him moan,
> And glimmering low on the dusky sky
> The hoard of gold goes racing by.

Norman played " The Farmer and the Fairies " for the first time on the piano at Losely, when his friend Avery Robinson was paying a return visit for Norman's stay at Forest Nook, Ontario. He had composed the setting for Henry Ainley, and Ainley gave the recitation at Broadcasting House in 1931, when Norman conducted the orchestra.

Perhaps it was Norman's daughter who missed Losely the most. She found it hard to part from " Neddy," and her pointer " John " ; and all the places where she knew she could find flowers : the back field on whose slopes the purple orchid grew in a mass, the ditches full of violets and primroses, the banks where the foxgloves rose ; and the hills where she picked bilberries and watched the gipsies.

CHAPTER XV

TEACHING

WE have seen that throughout his married life Norman had occasionally supplemented his income by giving piano, harmony, and composition lessons, and that in early days he taught for a time at a Highgate girls' school. In September 1924 he regularised these intermittent hours of teaching by joining the staff of the Royal Academy of Music as a Professor of Harmony and Composition, a post for which his great experience and knowledge of the technique of composition particularly qualified him. He also acted twice yearly as an examiner for the Associated Board of the R.A.M. and R.C.M. in their examinations up and down the country.

Norman had always had the gift of being able to write piano pieces for children, a talent by no means common or easy of acquisition. As early as 1908, Schott had published two easy pieces by him : one a " Gigue," which his son Patrick played very well,[1] and a dozen more were published between 1918 and 1921. In 1923 came his " Four Little Dances," written for his daughter and played by her at the age of seven. From 1926 onwards children's pieces by Norman were published nearly every year, among them " Four Tunes for the Sea," " Four Country Pictures," " The Sailor Boy," two sets of duets, and a little suite called " The King's House," which consisted of short pieces representing the members of a mediæval royal household : the heralds, the chamberlain, the minstrels, the astrologer, the jester, the huntsman, and so on. He also wrote a number of part-songs and unison-songs for schools.

At her school near Cranleigh, Yvonne used to hear other girls practising her father's " Four Little Dances," and sometimes, with much labour and difficulty, his " Hornpipe." The headmistress was a great admirer of Norman's music, and played the gramophone record of the " Call " from *Mary Rose* before school prayers, rather to Norman's amusement, for he could not see it was particularly appropriate ; however, the girls much preferred it to " O for the Wings of a Dove." On one memorable occasion Norman was called upon to give away the school prizes,

---

[1] Patrick went to school at Aldenham and later entered the service of Imperial Airways. In 1927 he married, and went out to Egypt to manage the aerodrome at Gaza.

including a certificate for the piano for his daughter. He was very embarrassed, but made an appropriate little speech, and of course charmed everybody.

The following draft, found among Norman's papers, of a talk which he was asked to give to another school—when and where is not known, but probably on one of his examining tours—shows how well he understood how to talk to the young and hold their interest :

Now, children, I am not going to make a long speech, or give you a lecture. I want to give you a few hints about exams and the preparation for exams. I shall also let you know some of the difficulties examiners have, so perhaps some of you will give *me* a few hints, too.

There are two important things about exams. One is nice and one is nasty. One either fails or succeeds. Now nobody likes to fail, do they? At the same time it is not at all a bad thing for some candidates to fail. If one fails because he or she lacks all talent and feeling for music, and is so discouraged that he or she gives it up as a bad job, that is probably a good thing, and the time spent on music will be much better spent on something else.

But it sometimes happens that a candidate who has musical feeling fails for some other reason. For instance, the pieces may be quite nicely played, but the scales, exercises, reading, and even time, may be so bad that it is not possible for the examiner, try as hard as he may, to give enough marks to give even a pass. It is often said that many failures occur owing to nerves and lack of confidence. This is sometimes the case, but the chief reason is usually lack of preparation. If a candidate has really thoroughly prepared the work, then nervousness may be responsible for not playing quite as well as he did at home, but it will not wholly spoil the performance. For instance, no nervousness is responsible for the failure of a candidate due to bad fingering, a total absence of musical expression, and entire ignorance of the formation of scales !

Now, we all want to obtain good marks, do we not? Well, the only way to ensure that is to have your work thoroughly and carefully prepared. You will then have on an armour which will successfully protect you from the Nerve Dragon. Do not forget that, however musical and fond of music you are, you cannot render it without having mastered the technical difficulties. A pupil once said to me that she was much too fond of music to bother with " those ugly scales and exercises." I assured her that her performances were a strange way of showing her love for it. Paderewski once said : " If I do not practise for a day I notice the difference in my playing ; if I don't practise for two days, my manager notices it ; and if I don't practise for three days, the public notices it ! "

Apropos of funny things said to me by pupils, here are two questions and the answers that were given to them :

Q. What is a double bar ?
A. A double bar is a bar which contains twice as many notes as the key signature.
Q. What is the difference between simple and compound time ?
A. In simple time the *odd* thing is a note and in compound time it is a beat.
And here is a story told me by a friend, a professor of piano. She said to the pupil : " This piece is by Norman O'Neill, who is coming to examine

8

you next week." The pupil looked very astonished and replied : " Oh—I thought all composers were dead ! "

In preparing candidates for examinations formerly, and the same fault is prevalent in those I examine to-day, I have always found the most common and serious fault is lack of rhythm. It seems to be almost a national fault in us. Now, to play out of time is really dishonesty in music ! And one must be honest in music just as one should be honest in everyday life. One must not rob a bar of a beat, or even half a beat, and not pay it back. You would not like me to borrow half-crowns from you to-night and then just fade away ! So it is in music. If one hurries a little in one bar, it must be made up by correspondingly slackening the speed, and vice versa. But to steal even a dot off a note and not give it back is not musically honest.

Rhythm seems to be the thing we English as a people lack, although I think we are just as honest, perhaps more so, than some of our very rhythmic neighbours, not only in the British Isles but on the other side of the Channel. When I have found a pupil greatly lacking in the sense of time, I have discovered that the following musical exercise is helpful to a fuller understanding of rhythm. I play on the piano any popular piece—a song, even a jazz—anything that happens to be familiar to him. I then write down some additional notes on a piece of music paper. These I get him to play at the top of the piano while I play below. In this way one begins to supplement the lack of sense of time, and one forces the pupil to share in the rhythm of a piece which he is far from being able to execute rhythmically alone.

Not long ago I addressed an audience of " listeners-in." Few of them had ever touched an instrument. Now, one of the reasons I like talking to you is that you are people who are learning to make your own music. Nobody can get the full measure of satisfaction from the art unless they know and play an instrument. The pleasure you will get from listening to musical performances, either in the concert hall or on the wireless, will be far greater than that of those listeners who have no practical knowledge of music.

There is good reason for saying that if the modern developments of producing music by mechanical means are going to have the effect of preventing people from making their own music, it will lead to a very serious state of things. But I am not at all pessimistic. When one thinks that to-day there are thousands of children, and young people, learning to play instruments seriously and well, I do not think there is much fear of any such disaster taking place. Only good should come of the mechanical reproductions which are bringing such a wide range of music to such vast numbers of people. At the same time, do not forget that these machines cannot take the place of the real thing.

You are part of that great audience that is growing up who will not only be " fond of music," as the saying goes, but who will have a real knowledge and understanding of it. This knowledge, however, you cannot attain unless you have some technical facility. The tediousness felt during the early stages of learning an instrument, and which tends to make the pupil discouraged, can be softened when he is given some slight notions of musical understanding. This keeps the interest in music awake. Musical help of this kind can also be given by what we call mechanical means—that is to say, by listening to good records and wireless. And the professor can often stimulate the pupil by playing attractive music to him or her. For although the dry technical side is important, the most important thing of all is musical understanding. We cannot all become great performers, but all those of us who have the desire to do so may become adequate players with enough knowledge of the art to have real understanding for it ; and then you will get great joy from the youngest but probably the greatest of the arts—the art of music.

At the R.A.M. Norman was recognised as an inspiring teacher. In the words of the Academy's own journal, he " immediately established himself as a master of his subject, alike with his colleagues as with his students." The understanding he showed for each pupil as an individual, and the human sympathy, encouragement and help he was always ready to give, were generally acknowledged.

In his teaching he made a point of imparting those qualities so conspicuous in his own compositions : clearness, coherence, form and musicality. Nothing ugly, diffuse, or " muddy " passed unheeded. To his relationships with his pupils he brought the qualities inherent in his nature : punctuality, good manners, dignity, friendliness, humour without familiarity ; and last, but not least, his irresistible charm. If he had been spared more years, his reputation as a teacher at the Academy would have become widely known.

CHAPTER XVI

" THUS MUCH OF MUSIC "

THOUGH Norman had written such appropriate music in the Italian style for *The Merchant of Venice*, it was not until 1931 that he had an opportunity of seeing Italy and Venice for himself. This presented itself in the form of a kind invitation from his friend Balfour Gardiner to accompany him and Frederic Austin on a cruise along the Dalmatian coast. After dining with the three composers at the Gare de Lyon in Paris, one night in April of that year, Adine and Yvonne enviously watched them being installed in their comfortable *wagon-lit*. Let Mr. Balfour Gardiner take up the tale :

We arrived in Milan at 11.30 and spent two hours in the town. Thence to Verona. Norman seemed a little disappointed, though of course he did not say so : if the holiday consists of sight-seeing like this, he thought, it will not be much fun. But I had purposely stopped at these places so that we might arrive at Venice at night, a wonderful experience. We emerged from the railway station not on to a street but on to the Grand Canal with its gondolas and motor-boats. Norman was enchanted. We put up at an excellent hotel, the Europe, and had great luck, for the next day was the national fête day and the Piazza San Marco was thronged with Fascists, military and civilians.

The same night we went to Trieste. Up early next morning, and by motor-coach over the hills to Fiume. At Susak, just over the bridge that divides Italy from Yugoslavia, we went aboard the *Llublyana*, a small coasting steamer, very comfortable and with pleasant passengers. We touched at Rub and Trogir and Split and arrived at Gravosa, the port of Dubrovnik (Ragusa), on the afternoon of April 24. For the next week the Hotel Excelsior Odak was our headquarters. Dubrovnik itself is a never-ending delight, but each day we went for an expedition : to Trebinje, to the Ombla, to Cavat, to Trsteno, and we went up to Cetinje by the famous winding road built by the Austrians. This is now a commonplace, but none the less wonderful for those who do it for the first time.

From Dubrovnik we took the steamer to Split, where we stayed the night : thence by train to the Plitvice lakes and to Zagreb and Salzburg. From Salzburg we went to Munich, and stayed at the Vierjahreszeiten : Clé Franckenstein entertained us with his usual magnificent hospitality, taking us out to Nymphenburg and giving us seats at the opera for *Gianni Schichi* and *Cassenoisette* and *Rosenkavalier*. Norman and Fred stayed on a couple of days—or rather, Fred did—Norman had to go back home : I myself went to the Black Forest.

Norman enjoyed the trip enormously. I think I may say he was one of the best travelling companions I ever knew, good-humoured, accommodating, with no tiresome ideas about the necessity of seeing all the " sights " and so on. I believe he always looked back with pleasure on those few weeks, as Fred and I do.

Mr. Frederic Austin writes :

New sights and sounds, ideal weather, and three long-intimate and congenial friends—what more delightful holiday could be imagined ? It was also, alas, to be a last golden aftermath of the happy years in which we, with other kindred creative spirits, had lived and worked, before the first world war had touched everything we had known with its disintegrating finger.

I first met Norman O'Neill in the little house in which he lived, newly married, in Edwardes Square. I was then setting out on my adventures as a singer, he on his as a composer. He was particularly armed, I remember, with the MS. full score of his overture to *Hamlet*—a work that not only bore definite signs of the dramatic gift that was later to make him the chosen composer for the theatre of his day, but had the sign-manual of one whose musical background was secure and whose style might easily have had an individual development in other directions.

In these days of panatropes and similar abominations, it is perhaps difficult to realise the then generally accepted view that an adequate orchestra was necessary in any properly organised theatre. That it was so was O'Neill's opportunity, as it had been Arthur Sullivan's and Edward German's before him. Of the long list of plays for which he wrote music, two examples particularly stand out in my mind—his music to *King Lear* and to Dunsany's *The Gods of the Mountain*. These productions gave him the opportunity of showing the " bigger fist " that he had at his command when needed, in addition to the poetry, piquant colour and easy grace that were more generally known as his particular characteristics.

His quite personal lyrical turn is delightfully shown in the group of songs published by the firm of Cary, and his large-scale setting of Keats's " La Belle Dame sans Merci " for baritone and orchestra is a glowing and impassioned piece of music.

O'Neill's sunny good-humour and ready *camaraderie* endeared him to his many friends, myself among them ; but there was a less-known side of him that from time to time came uppermost when, with an odd half-hour to spare, I used to stroll round to his house and go with him into his garden with its giant hollyhocks and foxgloves. There he would brood lovingly over his fish tank with its ingenious supply of running water—blood-brother to Mytyl and Tyltyl of *The Blue Bird*, for whom he wrote such fragrant, child-like music.

It is this gift of *camaraderie*, and Norman's continual willingness to help and advise others, that all his friends would wish to find stressed ; for this reason, the atmosphere of good fellowship at the Savage Club particularly appealed to him. Many of the best-known musicians of his time were, on one occasion or another, guests of the O'Neills on Sunday evenings at Pembroke Villas ; and Norman was always a welcome figure at social functions, such as the dinner to Edward German on his knighthood, or a certain famous lunch given by Elgar to his brother musicians.[1] He took the chair at the " Ladies' Night " of the

[1] Mrs. C. E. Blake, Elgar's daughter, writes : " My father had great admiration for Norman O'Neill and took a great interest in his work."

Savage Club at the Café Royal in 1932, when Mrs. Dod Procter was the guest of the evening.

When Siegfried Wagner came to England in 1930, to conduct some recordings, a few months before his death, the Columbia Gramophone Company, in order to show him something distinctively English, entertained him and his wife at an intimate supper at the Cheshire Cheese. Norman enjoyed that evening ; Adine sat next to Siegfried Wagner, talked French to him and thought him charming. His face bore a striking likeness to his father's, though he was of a different and slighter build. But he was on a strict diet and by no means well, so that his expression when the famous pudding appeared was the reverse of enthusiastic.

In the early 'thirties Norman again turned, after an interval, to song-writing, and these years saw the publication of " Jewels " (with words by Herbert Asquith), " May Lilies," " When May walks by," and " The Music of the Waves," by Sir Harold Boulton, for mixed-voice choir. In the theatre he was as busy as ever, but fortune was still inconstant. Much was hoped of the lavish production of *Little Catherine*, translated from the French by Mr. and Mrs. Vernon, which was seen at the Phœnix Theatre in November 1931, with Marie Tempest and Madeleine Carroll. The piece had its attractions, of which Norman's music was one, but, in the words of *The Times*, " the mystery of the play's mood and intention " overlay them. Nevertheless, Marie Tempest liked *Little Catherine* well enough to appear in an act of it at the special matinée in 1935 celebrating her golden jubilee on the stage.

At the end of January 1932 Norman regretfully severed his connection with the Haymarket, which had lasted, with one short interval, for twenty-two years. The further drastic reduction, for the sake of economy, in the size of his orchestra, and a succession of plays like *The First Mrs. Fraser*, which, though highly successful, did not require his special attention, were the main reasons for his departure ; and he felt on the whole that he might make better use of his talent elsewhere. His first engagement away from the Haymarket was to conduct his music for the successful revival of *The Merchant of Venice* at the St. James's in April 1932, in which Ernest Milton was such a memorable Shylock. Of this production Mr. Ernest Milton writes :

I shall always look back on *The Merchant of Venice* at the St. James's for his music alone—and for the warm stimulus I received when I nightly felt the presence of that grand, poetic man on the other side of the footlights.

XIV.—NORMAN O'NEILL, AGED FIFTY-THREE

XV.—THE "FRANKFORT GANG" GROWN UP

(*Left to Right*) Cyril Scott, Roger Quilter, Percy Grainger, Norman O'Neill.
A photograph taken at the Harrogate Festival in 1930.

All of his music was lovely, and I feel sure that his setting of "Tell me where is fancy bred" will take its permanent place in the heritage of deathless Shakespearean songs. . . .

Among the other productions of 1932 and 1933 for which he wrote music were *Man Overboard, Francis Thompson, Acropolis,* and *This Side Idolatry. Man Overboard,* in which Leon M. Lion and Emlyn Williams appeared, was an ingenious, imaginative, but perhaps rather long-winded play by Sutton Vane, which did not quite "come off." *Francis Thompson,* in which Ernest Milton played the name-part, was first produced at Kew and then transferred to the Royalty. Here Norman showed how fast he could work. He saw the play one Friday night at Kew, and by the following Monday evening, when there was a dress-rehearsal at the Royalty, he had written the whole score of three preludes and three interludes (twenty-four pages of music) for a trio.

Gladys Cooper and Raymond Massey acted in Robert E. Sherwood's *Acropolis,* an interesting play about the building of the Parthenon, which benefited by some artistic scenery by Aubrey Hammond. It had a moderate run at the Lyric Theatre. For the first time Norman's music was recorded and played on a panatrope, and he did not like this at all.

This Side Idolatry, which was produced in October 1933, with Leslie Howard and Margaret Rawlings, appealed to Norman more than any of these plays ; for it was written around a character, who interested him intensely—Shakespeare. To write a play about Shakespeare is extremely difficult, but this one by Talbot Jennings was skilfully contrived, and, as *The Times* said, the man was alive, " and without doing much violence to our preconceived notions, we may suppose him to be the kind of man that the real Shakespeare was." Perhaps Leslie Howard was miscast as the Bard ; at all events, the play did not last long. Norman and Leslie Howard had much in common, both in build, in distinction of features, and in charm of manner, and sitting together in the studio at Pembroke Villas they made a memorable pair. Howard suggested that Norman might write the music for his next film, *Smilin' Through,* and it is probable that, if he had lived, Norman's introduction to Hollywood would have come in this way.

However, Norman was now busy with some extremely congenial work, having signed a contract with Sir Oswald Stoll for a series of Shakespeare plays, to be produced by Colonel Stanley Bell. The first three plays chosen were *Julius Cæsar, The Merchant of Venice,* and *Henry V,* and they were produced at

the Manchester Hippodrome at Christmas 1933. Norman
came not unprepared to the first two plays, but he had to write
entirely new music for *Henry V*, and in Colonel Bell's words, " he
did a magnificent job and was a great factor towards the success
we had. . . . To my mind there has never been anyone quite
like Norman, both as a writer of stage music and a friend."

While in Manchester conducting *Henry V*, Norman wrote to
Elgar to sympathise with him in what was to prove his last
illness, and received the following reply from the nursing-home
at Worcester :

December 22, 1933.

My Dear O'Neill,—I was delighted to receive your letter, and it is
good news that you are in Manchester for such a big thing as *Henry V*. I am
very glad that they are giving your music with a real orchestra.

The announcement that I had gone home was premature ; I shall be here
for a long time yet.

I was delighted to see Delius in his home and am glad he allowed me the
privilege, although it involved 80 miles in a French taxi ; the prospect of
seeing him made the journey a light matter.

With kindest regards, Yours very sincerely,

Edward Elgar.

Elgar was allowed to leave the nursing-home early in 1934,
but he then got rapidly worse, and in February he died. His
visit to Delius at Grez was one of the last he paid to anyone,
and had been greatly enjoyed by them both. Little though he
dreamed it, Norman had also paid his last visit to his old friend
after his annual stay at Bagnoles that summer. Delius's niece
has memories of a " very jolly luncheon party," with the usual
excellent food and champagne, and of Norman sitting under a
tree " on a fine summer day, busily scoring music, all around
him glorious flowers and the peace of an old French garden."

On the back of Elgar's letter Norman scribbled in pencil
" 10-30 ock, Thursday Jan 11 to try voices—Jan 16 & 19, teach
supers 4 ock." He was back in London again from Manchester
by then, rehearsing the same three plays at the Alhambra.
Arrangements had been made for him to return to Manchester
later in the year for *Twelfth Night* and *The Merry Wives of Windsor*.
The back of Elgar's letter contains a note of something he had
in mind to transpose for the *Merry Wives*, and he had already
written some of his music for *Twelfth Night*.

The first performance of *Henry V* at the Alhambra went by,
with Godfrey Tearle a splendid Harry, Yvonne Arnaud an amusing Katharine. Then fate took a hand. In the late afternoon
of February 12, Norman set out from Pembroke Villas to go by
bus to Broadcasting House to conduct a rehearsal of a programme

of his Shakespearean music : the *Hamlet* overture, three sketches from *The Merchant of Venice*, four songs (sung by George Baker), and the first concert performance of his battle music and marches from *Henry V*. He got off the bus at the corner of Oxford Street and Holles Street, and was half-way across Holles Street when a small three-wheeled trade car, coming from Oxford Street, turned into the road behind him. He hesitated a moment and the driving mirror on the off-side of the " tri-car " struck him, so that he fell down and cut his head. " It was my fault," he said afterwards ; " I was thinking of my work."

The cut was nasty, but should not really have been serious. A lady who helped him, an entire stranger, wrote later to Adine : " I shall never forget the wonderful way your dear husband tried to pull himself together after the accident, and the most charming manner in which he thanked me for the little help I had given him." He was taken to hospital, where his head was bandaged. The hospital authorities wanted him to stay ; but he was still thinking all the time about his work, and he insisted on going home.

When his doctor saw him, later in the evening, it seemed as if he was getting over the concussion, and that no serious harm had been done. The next night he even went to the Alhambra and conducted the orchestra for *Henry V*, though the doctor thought he would have been better in bed. According to Colonel Bell, " he went into the orchestra at the beginning of the show in bandages, and would not come out at the interval for fear that I would insist on his going home." But after the performance he collapsed, and for the next three weeks the doctors fought a losing battle for his life.

Blood-poisoning had set in ; henceforth his mind became more and more clouded. The B.B.C. concert of his music on February 17 was taken by Julian Clifford, but though Adine offered to bring the wireless into his bedroom he had no wish to hear it. Yet his sense of duty still carried him on, and he made alterations to the *Julius Cæsar* music in bed. Days went by and he did not get better. Ernest Irving stepped gallantly into the breach at the Alhambra to conduct *Julius Cæsar*—a poignant experience, as Norman lay dying.

Eventually Norman was taken to a nursing-home, and there was an operation and a blood transfusion ; but it was too late. A clot of blood had formed, and on March 3 he died. It was eleven days before his fifty-ninth birthday.

Yvonne remembered that, before leaving for the B.B.C. on the day of the accident, he had played over his setting of " Come away Death," which he had intended to use for *Twelfth Night*. And on his piano Adine found in manuscript his last work as a composer. It was a setting of a lyric by Elizabeth Haddon, a girl of fourteen, which had the lines :

> Home of mine, when I am dying
> I'll return to you. . . .

Those who knew and loved Norman will agree that there was nothing quite like the shock of his sudden death, just as there had been nothing quite like his friendship. To many, who may perhaps have known of his accident but thought he was getting better, the news came with tragic abruptness when they read it in the newspapers or heard it over the wireless. Delius, according to Eric Fenby, was " heartbroken." The love that many felt for Norman could be sensed even in some of the formal obituaries in the morning papers ; but it shone clearly in little paragraphs here and there in the evening papers and weeklies. " He had such young eyes and such a ready, youthful smile," said one evening paper ; he was " a real good fellow," said another.

An inquest was necessary, and returned a verdict of " accidental death." At Golders Green the funeral service showed the range of Norman's activities and the width of his circle of friends : the Haymarket Theatre, the B.B.C., the " Phil," the R.A.M., the Savage Club—all were represented, and there were nearly a hundred wreaths. Several hundred letters came to Adine. A colleague at the R.A.M. said that " even the little lift-girl at the Academy was distressed and said, ' It doesn't seem true, does it ? ' " Two other sentences will summarise the thoughts of many others—one from Sir Henry Wood : " The whole world of musicians who knew him, and had the pleasure of working with him, loved him " ; the other from Dr. Vaughan Williams : " I first saw him years ago, when he was quite a boy—he seemed to me to keep his essential youth to the end."

At the next concert of the Royal Philharmonic Society, Mozart's Funeral Music was played in his memory ; and at the R.A.M. students' concert the funeral march from *Grania and Diarmid*, in honour of Elgar and of Norman.

A life so happy, both for himself and others, needs no laboured summary. Norman's friends had scarcely resigned themselves to the fact that he had gone when the first night of *The Merchant of Venice* took place at the Alhambra. It was a lovely revival, with some fine acting. " Not least," said *The Morning Post*, " the exquisite music composed by the late Norman O'Neill, whose death during the rehearsals was so bitter a loss to English music, lends the whole thing an atmosphere of romance." The reminder was timely. Not all of Norman had gone. He lived on in his music, as well as in the hearts of his friends.

In estimating his place in music, let us consider what he did. His earlier works, produced at the Queen's Hall, made, in Sir Henry Wood's words, " a great and a lasting impression." For incidental stage music he had a genius unique among English composers ; and many will say the same for his songs, too little known. " His work at the Haymarket set a standard of theatrical music," said *The Times* in his obituary notice, " which seemed likely to produce a widespread artistic reform until the modern mechanisms and the bad times together put an end to the old tradition. . . ." A writer in a weekly paper pointed out that Norman—

Died with his powers undiminished, for the music he was writing for the series of Stoll Shakespearean revivals was in his best style. That style was almost wholly individual. But if he had any musical affinity, it was with his great friend, Delius. " Delius's music is so tender," O'Neill remarked to me, and his own music was tender, too.

Norman would not have scorned this compliment. That, despite much search, he never found a libretto for an operetta that appealed to his careful taste, is our loss.

In April 1936 a little group met at Golders Green Crematorium, when Sir John Martin-Harvey, who had watched the beginning of Norman's career, unveiled a tablet to his memory. Mr. George Baker in an understanding tribute recalled Tyltyl's cry in *The Blue Bird*, " There are no dead . . ." and, thinking next of *Mary Rose*, said that Norman had gone over to the island, whither we too would follow when we heard the call.

The tablet designed by Albert Toft, a brother Savage who carried out the work as a labour of love, is placed in a small courtyard with a view on to the lily pond. It is of white stone with bronze low relief, and after recording the dates of Norman's birth and death, has this quotation from Shakespeare :

> In sweet music is such art :
> Killing care and grief of heart
> Fall asleep, or, hearing, die.

Appropriate though they are, we will not leave these as our last words, but remembering all the happiness Norman gave, and all the grace and loveliness that were in him, let us say with Plato : " Thus much of music, which makes a fair ending ; for what should be the end of music if not the love of beauty ? "

MUSIC TO STAGE PLAYS

By Norman O'Neill

[This paper was given to a meeting of the Musical Association, with Dr. W. H. Cummings in the chair, on March 21, 1911. In reading it, the date should be borne in mind.]

In England, more than in any other country, music has been constantly associated with the performance of stage plays. There is very early evidence of this. In the Miracle Play (1512) the minstrels are asked " To do their diligence " before the prologue, and at the end " To give us a daunce." Shakespeare relied on music to emphasise certain dramatic situations. No fewer than some three hundred times do his stage directions demand the employment of music. I do not speak of references to music on the part of his *characters*—these are frequent, always correct, and often jocular—but to actual demand for music, such as " Music plays," " Soft music within," and the like. Dr. Naylor in his interesting little work, *Shakespeare and Music*, declares that such stage directions as these appear no less than forty-one times, music during speeches seven times, and that eighteen times a march is required. Of songs, catches, dirges, trumpets, hautboys, countless examples are to be found in the plays. Very often Shakespeare makes quite subtle distinctions to suit the situation in his directions for music. In *King Lear* there are some interesting examples of this. The first appearance of Lear in regal state is heralded by a flourish of trumpets. Later on, in Scene 4, horns are directed to be played before his entrance. This is no doubt done with a view to denoting his lessened state. He has also just returned from hunting. This shows, I think, that more than a casual thought was given to the matter. Again, in *Lear*, in Act 4, we find the direction, " Soft music playing." Lear is on a bed asleep. That Shakespeare intended the music to continue through the scene and dialogue is evident, as the doctor refers to it in his lines, " Louder the music there." At this point the dramatist no doubt felt that the beautiful words of Cordelia, " O my dear father ! Restoration, hang thy medicine on my lips," would be greatly helped by the musical support. The very next scene opens with drums beating and soldiers marching, music very different in character from the " soft music playing " of the previous scene. This I feel sure was not mere accident, and that Shakespeare well knew the value of this contrast which at the same time connects the two scenes.

I will only quote one or two instances from *Hamlet* before passing on to other aspects of the subject. What could be more effective and sinister than the hautboys playing, probably some simple folk tune, before the play scene ; and again, the distant blare of trumpets which precedes the lines " the king doth wake to-night . . . and as he drains his draughts of Rhenish down the kettle-drum and trumpet thus bray out." Ophelia's songs, of which we still have the traditional tunes, the snatches of song by the grave-digger, each make their own particular effect. After Hamlet's death we have a march to precede the entrance of Fortinbras—again this strong feeling for contrast to be obtained by the music—and his order to the captains to bear Hamlet away, with the concluding words, " and for his passage the soldiers' music, and the rites of war speak loudly for him," all go to prove that Shakespeare well knew the value of music to help his dramatic effects and situations.

Another instance of Shakespeare's partiality for the hautboy and his undoubted feeling for its particular and sinister colour appears in *Antony and Cleopatra*. The stage direction is " Music of Hautboys *under* the stage." Antony has gone to supper, and the scene is before the palace with two soldiers on guard. The first soldier speaks : " Peace ! what noise ? Hark ! music i' th' air ! Under the earth," and so on. Shakespeare never introduced music without good reason, and will usually at the same time refer to it in the text, or when it is not referred to by one of the characters it is usually introduced in a perfectly natural way and at a point where music can be legitimately used. It may be of interest to remark that the instruments employed in Shakespeare's time in the theatre were, as far as is known, a combination of stringed instruments. Sometimes flutes and hautboys were added. Anything more than this in the way of a climax of sound was probably obtained by trumpets and drums.

Many a conductor in our smaller provincial theatres to-day has less than this at his disposal. In illustration of this perhaps you will allow me to tell the following story. I was once asked to write some music for a play which was to go on tour in our small towns. When I inquired what kind of orchestra I should write for, I was informed that in some places I might find twelve players ; this would be considered a great luxury and would only exist in a very prosperous theatre. In others I should constantly find only three players (pianoforte, cornet, and violin), and so it was necessary to write my music in such a way that it could be performed by any of these noble combinations. Considerable economy of instrumentation and material was necessary, I need hardly say.

I think I have said enough to show that music in connection with plays was in use in Shakespeare's time, and I look upon him to a great extent as the originator of our stage music. It is most unfortunate that none of this instrumental music has come down to us. But as I have already pointed out, some of the Elizabethan songs have carried down with them the tradition of their original tunes.

I have not time here to go fully into the whole history and development of theatre music, and I do not think it would be of very great interest if I had. Coming down to times within the memory of many musicians, I should like to mention Hatton's music written for Charles Kean's Shakespearean and other productions in the " 'fifties." These were, as far as I know, the first productions of modern times in England in which a well-known musician of the day was specially engaged to write special music for a play. This has, in our own day, become a regular practice. Most of our composers have written music for plays at some time or other. It is to Sir Henry Irving, who did so much to improve the artistic conditions of the theatre, that we are indebted for this. He saw the need of something better than the so-called " hurries," " tremolos," and sentimental hymn-like tunes which were being served up again and again in our theatres to an easily imposed-upon public. I was too young at the time to form any definite opinion as to the actual musical value of the Lyceum music, but one of my first great musical impressions was at a performance at that theatre.

Irving gave commissions to many young composers of his day, notably to Edward German, whose work places him in the front rank of composers who have written for the theatre. Sullivan's music to *Macbeth*, *The Foresters* (Tennyson), and *King Arthur* was all highly successful ; and the first-mentioned contains some of his best work ; into *Macbeth*, Sullivan put some of the strongest music he ever wrote. These were all produced by Irving, as well as *Henry VIII*, with music by Edward German. Apart from the well-known and charming dances, this work contains some of the most successful and characteristic music ever written for our theatre. German's style lends itself particularly well to this form of composition. Many other of our composers have also written music for plays, notably Elgar (*Grania and Diarmid*), Parry (*Hypatia*), Stanford (*Becket*, *Queen Mary*, etc.), Mackenzie (*Ravenswood* and *The Little Minister*), Coleridge-Taylor (*Herod*, *Faust*, etc.)

For the purpose of this paper I will classify music for the theatre under three heads. The first : Incidental music—which may or may not be specially composed for the play. The second : *Entr'actes* and Interlude music. The third : Music which is specially written for a play, and which is an essential part of the production.

The term " incidental music " is sometimes, and I think correctly, applied to marches, dances and songs which are incidental to the action of the play, but it is also applied to what is called " Melodrame,"—that is, to music which accompanies the dialogue and reflects the feeling and emotion of the spoken lines, instances of which I will give you shortly. Under this heading I would put such music as we hear with melodramas and dramas of the old school, such as *The Lyons Mail*, *The Bells*, *The Corsican Brothers*, and in the Lyceum and provincial dramas. Here the music plays a subsidiary part. It usually accompanies the most sentimental passages in the play, and plays a part similar to that of the limelight man, following the hero and heroine most obstinately. But the villain, too, will have his little bit of *tremolo* to help him along on his evil path. This type is usually most primitive in construction. It consists of an eight-bar phrase repeated *ad libitum* during a speech. And this proceeding will take place many times during an evening, so that it is very often heard forty or fifty times in the course of a play. Its use, if it can be so called, is usually to remind the audience of a previous situation. When the hero lies in prison, for instance, memories of the " old home " and his first meeting with the heroine are called up, and of course the old tune turns up too. I need hardly say that both drama and music of this class have no great artistic value. The music is simply called in to bolster up the weakness of the drama. It is used to stimulate (by what I may call unfair means) the imagination of the audience, and to help the actor in what for him might be some rather dangerous moments. It is supposed to be easier for an actor to " hold " his audience under these conditions than it is when he has to do all the work himself. This is, I think, one of the reasons why this type has survived so long. I do not think audiences particularly care for it, for I have a high opinion of the theatre public ; it is the actor who clings to this tradition of melodrama. Luckily, we do not get much of it in our first-class theatres, but if one goes to the suburbs and provinces one will still find it, and I am afraid it will die hard. Particularly barbarous is it when some well-known melody is taken and misused *ad lib.* in this way. I have been told that one well-known actor has Raff's " Cavatina " played over and over again during the Balcony scene in *Romeo and Juliet*. More modern music has also been ill-treated in this way. In a pantomime this winter a theme of Tschaikovsky's, taken straight out of a symphony, was played several times during the evening as an incidental number.

It is appalling to think that composers and publishers are powerless to prevent this. I suppose, so long as the music is played from printed parts, there is nothing to prevent it, and we may expect to hear a phrase from Debussy's *Pelléas and Mélisande* accompanying the entrance of the Demon King ! It is dreadful to think to what lengths an enterprising pantomime-maker might go. Let us rather have the old type, the constantly repeated and insignificant eight-bar phrases.

But I do not wish to convey to you that music of this kind is always without merit. I will mention two well-known plays, *The Only Way* and *The Corsican Brothers*. The music to the latter has become almost traditional with the pit and gallery, and I have heard them sing the famous ghost theme with the orchestra. This is not a great melody, and has no particular musical value, but it certainly fits the situation. You will no doubt remember the ghost of one brother appears to another. The lights go down, the music starts in true melodramatic fashion, but still it holds the audience. Very much of the same type is the music to *The Only Way*, which as a means of welding together the action has undoubted value, and the short preludes and incidental numbers are always appropriate enough in their way. This brings me to a conclusion which I shall later enlarge upon, that it is not always so much the intrinsic value of the music as its appropriateness and aptness which make it successful from the theatrical point of view. I do not say, of course, that music of a higher order may not have these qualifications also. Indeed, it constantly has.

I have tried to show that music to melodramas is usually of a most primitive kind, the numbers, or eight-bar phrases, more or less appropriate, being repeated *ad lib.* through long speeches without any regard for the changes of thought and expression in the dialogue. This repetition has no doubt become a custom on account of the difficulty of measuring the length of speeches and stage business, and fitting music to them. If eight bars are repeated *ad lib.*, as long as music is wanted, it greatly simplifies the work of the composer, although it may exasperate some members of the audience. So far as London is concerned, and at any rate in our first-class theatre, this old-fashioned and inartistic type is practically extinct. Its long life can only be explained in one way, I think : the ignorance of the stage of some musical directors, and the primitive view of music taken by some actors. Happily the conditions are changing, and the composer to-day, who has knowledge and experience, will find as much sympathy, intelligence, and understanding for his work in the theatre as he will elsewhere. Music is no longer treated in the haphazard way it was formerly, and every musical effect will be as carefully prepared and rehearsed as the rest of the performance. The public, I think, have very little idea of the amount of thought, care and time spent on one of the modern productions seen on the London stage, which to them appear so simple when seen from the front of the house. A lady once wrote to me that she was getting up a performance, in the parish room, of a poetical play by Stephen Phillips for which I had written music for a performance in London. " We have an orchestra in our theatre," she wrote, " and we should much like it to play your music to the play as we are anxious to have our performance as like the one I saw in London as possible, and my husband thinks that if we had the music it would be a great help. Our orchestra consists of a piano, and we sometimes have a violin, which we hope to get again." I quote this story merely as an instance of the knowledge an ordinary member of the public has of the inner workings of this form of composition.

Under the heading of what I have called *Entr'acte* music, I would put music which is played between the scenes and acts of plays, and which does not accompany the action of the play. There may be no call for music during a play, but it may be necessary to have music during a quick change of scene. In some theatres an effort is made to have such music in keeping with the play. Effective and suitable music between the scenes can be of artistic value ; especially if there is an entire change of sentiment from the one scene to the other, the music can in more ways than one fill up the gap. I recollect an effective instance of this in Galsworthy's *Strife*, a modern play in which there is, of course, no incidental music. A short musical interlude played during a change of scene seemed to me exactly the right thing in the right place. This, I think, was specially written by Mr. Crook for the situation. But in a case of this kind there is, of course, no reason why a composition which has not been specially written should not be chosen, that is to say if the right piece for the particular situation, with the right sentiment, can be found. But as I have already pointed out this is rather a dangerous proceeding, on account of the associations which are inevitably bound up in our minds with any well-known pieces of music.

9

In many theatres the *Entr'acte* music is kept more or less in keeping with the play. Thus we have in a serious play music of a more or less serious nature, and in a light comedy music of a lighter nature. I am certainly in favour of this, although, if carried too far, it is apt to defeat its own end. Some people hold, however, quite the opposite view and think that the *Entr'acte* music should be in direct contrast to the play, the idea being to keep up the spirits of the audience, and play them galops and two-steps, barn-dances and marches, in the *entr'actes* of a farce or a serious play. The galops are certainly more suitable to a farce than to a serious play, but, to me, the curtain rising on an act of *The Wild Duck* to the last bars of the latest comic song has something about it that is a little absurd.

The experiment has been tried of having quartets and quintets by the great masters played as *entr'actes* in some theatres. Personally, I cannot see the reason for this. First, music of this kind seems utterly out of place in a theatre. The quartets of Beethoven, Brahms or Schubert can by no stretch of imagination be termed theatre music. But there is another and more practical reason against this. Those people who are really fond of chamber music, and would probably like to listen, are unable to do so on account of the noise made by others who quite naturally wish to talk about the play in the interval and do not care a rap about the music one way or the other. I think the only place where it is possible to play music of a more serious nature is at the beginning of the programme, before the people of the stalls and dress-circle arrive.

England is one of the few countries where it is usually deemed necessary to have music between the acts of all plays. This may or may not be a good thing ; but I am not going to decry it, for it gives a fixed means of livelihood to good orchestral players. This is, I think, at any rate for a musician, reason enough to tolerate music between the acts of plays, which some people, who are always anxious for us to imitate the foreigner, are so desirous of abolishing. Let us by all means have music in our theatres, but let it be suitable and appropriate. We do not want barn-dances or symphonic poems, but there is a great deal, and good music too, which can be played, and which can be enjoyed by the ordinary theatre public. Perhaps you will allow me to quote from my own experience at the Haymarket. There are certain pieces which constantly get a round of applause, and they are not always those that are the best known. I have played an unknown eighteenth-century piece after the " Barcarolle " from *Tales of Hoffmann*, and have had a round of applause for each.

Before I pass on to the most important part of my paper, I should like to say that it never seems to have struck composers to write *entr'acte* music, or even an overture, to any of our modern plays. Why, for instance, should a composer not be inspired to write a set of movements to Mr. Shaw's *Man and Superman*? I do not mean only for performance in the theatre, for the orchestral material there is usually limited, but also for the concert-room. It seems to me that here there is material ready to hand which should appeal to the modern composer of programme music. In the case of a well-known play he would have the advantage of a large section of the public knowing the poetic basis of his work without reference to "programme notes," and opportunity of performance in the theatre as well as in the concert-room.

I now come to the third and most important type : Music which is an essential feature of a play. In this class I would not, of course, place what are known as " musical plays " and " musical comedies." I have no place for them here.

Under this heading I would place Mendelssohn's *Midsummer Night's Dream* music ; Edward German's music to *Henry VIII* ; Humperdinck's music to the *Königskinder* ; Grieg's to *Peer Gynt* ; and Bizet's to *L'Arlesienne*. In all of these the successful performance of the play is to a very great extent dependent on the music. And in at least four of the above cases the music has become as celebrated as the play, and no performance could well be given without the music associated with that particular play. Certainly, both in the case of *L'Arlesienne* and *Königskinder* the music has kept the play before the French and German public. I will first take the French work. This consists of overture, *entr'actes*, and what is known as melodrame or incidental music. Bizet also makes very effective use of a chorus and a small orchestra on the stage. This orchestra accompanies the choral numbers which are all behind the scenes. He thus avoids the difficulty of combining a hidden chorus with orchestra in front of the stage. I think we all have experienced the dangers of this at the opera. *L'Arlesienne* is to my mind one of the most perfect examples of the play with music. The atmosphere and feeling of the play are faithfully followed throughout, and quite extraordinary sympathy for the emotions through which the characters are passing is shown in the music which accompanies the dialogue.

Humperdinck's *Königskinder*, I think, contains some of the most charming music this composer has written. In it he has attempted to measure the dialogue and music so exactly that it is necessary for the actors to be musicians if his idea is to be correctly carried out. He gives the dialogue in the score in this way. A rhythmic vocal part, as it were, is written. This of course is not to be sung, but to be spoken in time with the music. This involves considerable musicianship on the part of the actor, and apart from that is a severe handicap to him. When I heard this work in Germany, the chief parts were taken by singers whose acting was by no means on a high level, although they managed to keep with the music. This, I must say, cannot be looked upon as a successful experiment. Incidental music must be a mere accompaniment to the play. In the *Königskinder* the dialogue was an accompaniment to the music, and greatly as I admire it, it was not satisfactory in practical performance. Humperdinck has since used his music to the play in an opera of the same name, which I think shows he came to the same conclusion.

Mendelssohn's *Midsummer Night's Dream* is well known to everybody, and Edward German's delightful *Henry VIII* music has been heard by everybody interested in this form of art. The dances are of course well-known, but there is a great deal of charming incidental music that can only be heard with the play. The charming trio, " Orpheus with his lute," is an instance of a composer creating exactly the right atmosphere, and again of Shakespeare's extraordinary feeling for the introduction of music at the right moment into his dramatic scheme.

In all realistic plays, and I would place such works as *Hamlet* or *Lear* in this category, the introduction of music should only occur at such points as Shakespeare demands it, or where it is quite natural and reasonable to introduce it. The promiscuous introduction of music into a play of Shakespeare seems to me quite inartistic and pointless. There must always be some good artistic reason, or actual necessity, for music. In my opinion very little music is required during the action of most of Shakespeare's plays, but almost all of them give the composer opportunities of expressing himself appropriately, if, perhaps, at no great length.

In fantastic plays, in which there is a fairy or mystic, or even supernatural element, music may, and of course constantly quite rightly does, play an important and essential part, and can, I think, quite legitimately accompany the dialogue. Music should step in where the play itself, the actors and the stage effect, can no longer carry on the illusion. And it is just in such cases that the composer can work wonders and create atmosphere and effects which may be unique in their way.

Any play which it would be impossible to perform without music would belong to this type : a play in which songs and dances are essential, a play in which dramatic effects rely on the music for their adequate expression, a play in which effects of scenery and lighting are illustrated by music. I think it is evident that this is the type of work which gives the greatest scope to the musician, and I will now endeavour to give some idea as to the ways and means, the difficulties, and the methods employed by composers and producers of plays in which music plays an important part.

When a play in which the music is to be an important feature is to be put upon the stage, the composer usually meets the author and the producer and discusses where it will be advisable to introduce music. The producer or *metteur en scène* of a play draws up a plan of the whole action in every detail, the scenic effects, and so forth, which he intends to employ. These will greatly determine the spirit and atmosphere of the production. It is not enough for a composer only to know the play through and through, but he must also be in close touch with the exact spirit in which the work is to be given. Where music is to accompany the dialogue he must, before writing any music, know the *tempo* of the speeches, the pauses and business to be introduced, so that his music may coincide in the minutest detail with the stage rendering of the play. He will otherwise find his musical effects clashing or coming in the wrong place. Where music accompanies the action and there is no dialogue, as for instance in a procession or entrances of characters, most careful adjustment is necessary, the producer and composer working together and arranging the time that any such effect or business will take on the stage. Where there is no dialogue, the stage business should be timed to the music. Where there is dialogue, the music should be timed to the stage. It is obviously much easier for the composer to accompany the actors in speeches than it would be for actors to follow the music. This is where, to my mind, *Königskinder* failed. The composer should be in touch with the producer when the whole production is worked out on paper, and then make his own scheme of the music. The difficulties are many, and unless the composer is in sympathy with the producer the chances of a successful result are very small. It is essential they should work together and understand exactly the effects they each desire to obtain.

To my mind music which accompanies the spoken words should be as unobtrusive as possible and not, strictly speaking, melodic. The feeling of the words is often better followed in the general harmonic scheme than by any clear-cut melody. An apt chord or turn of phrase is often more suggestive than a defined melody, which is often distracting when accompanying spoken prose. The musical accompaniment to a speech should steal in and steal out so quietly that the audience are no more aware of it than they are of some subtle change in the stage lighting. Bizet is most successful in his treatment of the melo-drame in *L'Arlesienne,* the music often beginning with one or two pianissimo violin notes *con sordini* and fading away again in the same way.

I do not wish to give you the impression that in music for the stage melody has no place. On the contrary, no successful incidental music (or any other for that matter) can be devoid of melody and thematic material. I only feel that clearly defined tunes in conjunction with the dialogue are out of place. When a running accompaniment of music is required for a long stretch of dialogue, the exact time of each speech, the pauses, entrances, and exits must all be carefully measured. In illustration of this, I will quote from a manuscript of a play to which I wrote the music. The scene opens with an Irish folk-song, at the close of which there are two lines of dialogue (twenty seconds), then a phrase of the song again, four lines of dialogue, at the end of which there is some business (half a minute), and so on. In this way I was able to time my music to the scene, throughout the whole of which music was played. As soon as the actors were word-perfect we rehearsed with the pianoforte, and so the music grew with the production. Even if they took a sentence a shade faster or slower it was an easy matter to accompany them so long as they kept to the originally arranged scheme of pauses and business. Of course, final touches are always made at rehearsal, and for that reason it is as well to have as many re-hearsals with pianoforte as possible before the play is taken with orchestra.

I will give you an instance of a musical number which only accompanies the action when there is no dialogue spoken, from Mr. Lyall Swete's scheme for the production of Maeterlinck's *The Blue Bird.* It is the entrance of the Fairy in the first Act : " Two loud knocks arrest the two children who are dancing round the room. Mytyl says, ' It's Daddy ! ' The music begins. The door opens slowly ; the music continues. The Fairy appears standing in the doorway. She walks slowly forward. The door shuts on the last note of the music." Knowledge of the size of the stage was of course necessary, but otherwise it was an easy matter to write the music when the business was clearly defined in this way. But it is not every author or producer who takes the trouble to work out his scheme so completely on paper beforehand. Sometimes a great deal is left until rehearsals begin. This, of course, makes it very much harder for the composer, as he is working more or less in the dark until within perhaps two or three weeks of the first performance, and he has often to alter and rearrange his music at the eleventh hour. This is most unsatisfactory. A very celebrated author once wrote to me, asking me to write some music for a short play, thirty-six hours before the first performance. " We rehearse to-morrow at 10.30," he wrote (this was the evening before ; I got the letter by the last post), " and if you could look in you would see what I want." I need hardly say I refused the offer, as it was quite impossible to write the music, have it copied and rehearsed, in the time.

One of the practical difficulties for the composer to overcome as best he may is in the case of music for a change of scene. Very often it is impossible for a stage-manager to tell within half a minute how long his change is going to take, and a slight accident may delay him. Even at the last dress rehearsal the composer may find that his interlude is too short, and that the change takes longer than was at first anticipated. By repeating a section he may find the effect he desires to get on the rise of the curtain is spoiled. For this reason, for a risky change of scene it is as well to have the music too long rather than too short, and the safest plan is to have a repeat *before* the end of the number which can be made in case of emergency. You will perhaps wonder how the conductor is to know when the stage is ready for the next scene after a change. In most theatres where music is considered seriously, the conductor and stage-manager have a system of communication by light signals, the stage-manager signalling to the conductor when the scene is ready, and the conductor replying with his light for the rise of the curtain. If the conductor does not get the light which signifies " all's well," he makes his repeat, the stage-manager switching on his message as soon as he is ready, and the conductor going straight on to the end of the number, giving light for the curtain at the proper place.

When music accompanies dramatic action without dialogue each movement of the actors must be timed to the music, and not only is a great deal of rehearsal usually necessary if the effects are at all elaborate, but what is sometimes more difficult to obtain, mutual sympathy between them and the conductor is essential. Sometimes, as in opera also, the best effects are those

which are the most simple. Such effects as the introduction of
a chorus behind the scenes, or a stage orchestra in conjunction
with the orchestra in front, are all hard to obtain in the theatre.
They are, of course, most effective if well arranged. We have
all probably heard the stage trumpet come to grief in *Carmen*,
or the " Sirens " sing anything but alluringly in *Tannhäuser*. In
L'Arlesienne Bizet avoids this danger by having a small stage
orchestra to accompany his hidden chorus. But the dramatic
situation will not always allow of that. There are other devices,
with which I need not trouble you now, by which such combinations as hidden voices and distant trumpets can be effectively
and safely accompanied by the orchestra.

In my opinion the orchestra in a theatre should always be
hidden from the public. Not only is it most distracting for the
audience to have the lights and movements of the players and
conductor between them and the stage, but it greatly adds to
the illusion if the music is heard and not seen. The best arrangement is for the orchestra to be sunk and covered in with palm
leaves, such as are used at His Majesty's Theatre and at the
Haymarket. Another reason why it is a great advantage to have
a covered orchestra is that it enables the conductor and performers to have proper lights. It is the custom in theatres where
the orchestra is open to use violet, or blue, lights in order that
there shall be less reflection on to the scene. This means that
the conductor is practically in semi-darkness and the music of
the players badly lighted. And as you sometimes have players—
deputies—reading at sight, and unable to see either the conductor or the music distinctly the result is often disastrous ! The
covered-in orchestra, of course, to a certain extent deadens the
sound, but it enables the composer to score very much more
richly in incidental music without running the risk of drowning
the voices of the actors. All music that actually accompanies
the spoken lines should, in my opinion, be mainly scored for
strings, which I think mix far better with the human voice than
do wood-wind instruments. Harps, horns and timpani—softly,
of course,—can also be used effectively, and, to quote Bizet again,
the lower notes of the flute. The fact that the clarinet is not a
suitable instrument to accompany the human voice was first
brought home to me by Martin-Harvey. I had written for the
solo clarinet in the accompaniment of a speech of his. In rehearsal, he stopped when he heard this. " Is that a clarinet ? "
he said. " Yes," I replied. " Oh, it sounds like a caricature of
my voice ! " And this is just the danger with reed instruments.
Horns, harps, and even the brass and percussion can be used in

melodrame, but for ordinary purposes the string orchestra is the best, and with regard to the wind, as they say in the Instrumentation primers, " these beautiful instruments should be used sparingly." As soon as music to the spoken lines becomes too obtrusive it defeats its own end. It is very often impossible for the conductor or the actor to tell if the music is too loud or too soft. The right balance can only be obtained from the theatre. Personally, I always listen to the music from the dress circle before the first performance.

It is often expected of the conductor that at a moment's notice in a performance he can step in and save the situation. For instance, there may be some music to bring some characters on to the stage. Perhaps they are late, and do not appear until the music is nearly over. To avoid an awkward stage wait of this kind some conductors always have " emergency repeats " in their scores. An amusing story is told of a well-known conductor who, on finding himself in a predicament of this kind, and no more music to play, leaned over to his 'cellos with the remark : " Tremble, boys, *ad lib.*," and thus filled up the pause until the late-comer arrived on the scene !

When a great deal of music occurs during the action of a play, I am not in favour of having long preludes to the acts. A short prelude with the lights lowered in the theatre is much more likely to produce the desired effect than a long *entr'acte* to which nobody will feel inclined to listen. If the theatre be thrown into darkness at the commencement of the music the audience are at once in a receptive mood. The composer should in a few bars endeavour to express the feeling of the coming scene, and the curtain rise on the last notes of his little prelude, thus as it were completing a circle of light and sound. The sudden putting out of lights in the theatre is in itself so ominous that obviously this proceeding is only in keeping with certain situations. For others it is more effective to lower the house lights gradually, and with the aid of the music to lead the attention of the audience to a gradually disclosed scene.

This brings me to the vexed question of what is the best orchestral combination to use in the theatre. There are two difficulties, one of which it is practically impossible to overcome, viz., the long, narrow shape of the theatre orchestra pit ; the other being the limited space at one's disposal. There are few theatres where it is possible to seat more than thirty players comfortably. And it must be borne in mind that twenty-six players with elbow-room will probably give you a better effect than thirty cramped and packed close together. Personally, I very much object to an orchestra in which there are as many wind players as strings. So often, in the theatre, music which has been scored for an orchestra of at least fifty is played with three trombones, trumpets, horns, and full wood-wind, against which struggle seven or eight violins, two violas, and two violoncellos. To my mind, it is far better to do with less wind and brass, and to get something like a proper balance between wind and strings. I will not lay down any hard-and-fast rule, but for ordinary purposes an orchestra of, say, twenty-six performers should, I think, be constituted in this way :

4 first violins,	2 flutes,
3 second violins,	1 oboe,
2 violas,	2 clarinets,
2 violoncellos,	1 bassoon,
2 double-basses,	2 horns, 2 trumpets,

and one trombone or harp and celesta (one player), one percussion.

This, at any rate to my mind, is the minimum of string players possible with this amount of wind, and even then they must be first-rate performers, and must have no dummies amongst them. The harp is more essential in a small orchestra than in a large one. It makes just this difference, I think, it turns what we call a " theatre band " into a little orchestra.

But twenty-six performers are a comparative luxury. For a run of a play in which there is no music, and during which the orchestra is only required in the *entr'actes*, a conductor may consider himself lucky if his management allows him eighteen or even sixteen players. For ordinary purposes an orchestra of eighteen performers should be constituted thus :

4 first violins,	1 oboe,
2 second violins,	1 clarinet,
1 viola,	1 bassoon,
2 violoncellos,	2 horns,
1 bass,	1 trumpet,
1 flute,	

and percussion. Of course with only a small orchestra the conductor will find it necessary to arrange nearly all the standard works, and in many cases practically re-score them for his combination of instruments. Many good arrangements of works by the great masters are published, but in numerous cases they fall short of the ideal, as the publishers insist that they be arranged in such a way that they can be played with some degree of effect by six or eighty performers.

ORIGINALITY IN MUSIC

By Norman O'Neill

[This paper is dated December 1927, and was read to the Incorporated Society of Musicians. Norman illustrated it by playing appropriate passages on the piano.]

SOMEBODY to whom I mentioned the chief points of this paper the other day said he thought it should be called *un*originality in music. You shall decide. But I assure you that the un-originality will be found in the paper itself, and not in the music I talk about. As the title *is* " Originality in Music," it may not be out of place to make a few introductory remarks on the origin and development of the art. I hope those to whom these remarks are ancient history will bear with me for the moment.

Music is really the most modern of the arts. It is not often realised how modern it is in the form we have it presented to us to-day. But it *is* brought home to some of us rather forcibly how new it is when we listen to some of the so-called modern music we hear. On the other hand again, some of it is so barbarous that we might be deluded into thinking it was of ancient origin.

Two thousand years ago painting and sculpture had many finished masterpieces. Music, on the other hand, was in a very primitive and incomplete condition. Eight hundred years ago music-makers had not got the means of putting down notes of unequal length. Such modern devices as bar lines were not thought of until four hundred years later. The employment of the bar dates from about the beginning of the sixteenth century. The works of Tallis, Byrd and Gibbons were all published without bars. I think Henry Lawes was the first Englishman to employ them. To-day attempts have been made by some composers to return to the barless age, a sort of musical prohibition which is surely only placing further difficulties in the way of adequate performance.

As I have already said, when, in the other arts, great works were being produced, music could hardly be written down. The history of notation is highly interesting : from its beginning with primitive signs to the elaborate system of the present time. No doubt the ancients had some sort of music—melody, perhaps consisting of the imitation of the songs of birds, a proceeding that has not been ignored by the composers of the past as well as of the present. I will try and make clear later what a great rôle imitation has played in the evolution of musical composition.

Sir Hubert Parry said that these actual melodies of the ancients lasted through the ages between the collapse of the great states of old times, such as Greece and Rome, and the days when our modern European states were developing towards their present condition. I do not know what authority he had for saying this, but it seems sound. Anyway, no doubt the birds sang all the time—up to the time when Wagner heard a blackbird sing in the Bavarian highlands.

It has been held that music, of all the arts, is the one that has the least connection with Nature. Mill said " of all the arts music is the most remote from positive reality." And Riemann said, " music borrows its data from a world far distant from that from which the other arts borrow theirs." In the early stages of music-making the natural sounds, the noises made by blowing through a pipe, striking wood against wood, the sound of running water and the rhythm of the sea, to mention only a few, must have had great influence on the composers. Music is a language used by composers to express their emotions. It springs at once from the will as an independent idea. Its appeal is to the inner consciousness. Music is at once, should be at once, intelligible of itself, needing no externals to mediate between it and the understanding. In one of his prose writings Wagner draws a parallel between the world of dreams and the world of music.

It was not until the eleventh century that the first attempts to write down music were made, and then only by signs to aid the memory. It was long after that the first attempt at part-writing was made—the beginning, in fact, of harmony. Then, even at that early stage, rules began to be made, those stumbling-blocks to progress which even to-day are felt. How many composers have been abused in their lifetime for breaking rules ! But daring must not be mistaken for originality. Everybody who breaks rules is not necessarily a genius. It sometimes requires more courage not to break them. But assuredly the great pioneers have been the greatest breakers of these so-called rules and conventions.

All advances in music have been made by accepting what has been condemned by recognised artistic authorities. In early days only the simplest of combinations were allowed to be used. To-day, and let us be glad of it, or not, a composer will use more dissonances in one bar than an early Italian or Flemish composer used during his whole lifetime. It is not so very long ago that consecutive fifths were looked upon with horror by all self-respecting musicians. In a very well-known treatise on harmony published only forty years ago (and, I regret to say, still used), the author writes a row of fifths, saying : " they are forbidden " ; he then adds the octaves to the same set of consecutive fifths, remarking : " nor is it any better if we add the octave, hence octaves are forbidden ! " The idea of progressions consisting of intervals of the 7th or 9th was quite out of the question. They were thought to be ugly, and no doubt were ugly to the ears of musicians of the time. We owe a debt to the great composers who gradually, step by step, broke down these traditions, thus advancing their art.

It seems that music is freer to-day. Musicians are more tolerant towards innovations than they formerly were. Fifty years ago—no, less than that—a Schönberg could hardly have walked with safety on Unter den Linden in Berlin. Such attacks as were made on Wagner's music by some of his contemporaries would hardly occur to-day. I hope this is not the result of indifference, but of a broader and more tolerant outlook.

Generally speaking, it was between the middle of the fifteenth century and the end of the sixteenth that the modern art of music was founded. Its foundations stretched far back. It is a thing to be proud of that our John Dunstable, who lived early in the fifteenth century (he died in 1450) was generally looked upon as the founder of this " new art." The scale, then consisting of ecclesiastical modes, was a modification of an arrangement invented in 1024 (known as Arezzo's). The sounds of two hexa-chords were sung to the UT-RE-MI-FA-SOL-LA, and the notes of the entire octave were known as A.B.C.D.E.F.G. The first step towards modern music arose from Descant, the art of combining melodies. Music up to the end of the sixteenth century was polyphonic, since then it has more or less been replaced by homophony.

In the Middle Ages Italy was the world's centre of art, but church music there was mostly made by Dutch and Belgian musicians. It is known that English musicians were amongst them, and that Dunstable and his followers migrated to and were known in Italy. And there their work had fruitful influence.

Probably the most distinguished composer in Italy of that period—I am now speaking of 1450–1500—was Josquin de Prez. His music was even known in England at Henry's court. This age was a golden one for music, both here and in Italy. After Josquin, the church music in Italy fell upon evil days. The clergy, seeking popularity, caused secular tunes to be introduced and set to the words of the Mass. The congregation, not knowing the Latin, and associating the popular words with the music, often joined in with the choir. The same sort of thing has been attempted in our own time, with equally comic results, and not only by the Salvation Army, I regret to say. Mr. Bernard Shaw tells how he once went into a celebrated Ethical Church and heard them singing " Oh may I join the choir invisible " to the tune of " Onward, Christian Soldiers," the rhythm of the words and music not tallying in the least !

Soon came a great figure—Palestrina—to restore dignity and beauty to Church music. He was rightly called " the saviour of Church music." Although choral music was in a fairly advanced state, at that time instrumental music was in a primitive condition. Instruments were still imperfect. Unaccompanied vocal music held its own. A group of composers after Palestrina tried to combine the two. But they had no model to copy, nothing to imitate, or to influence them. They had to start again at the beginning, as it were. But it was a beginning, and the beginning of great things to come.

In modern times we had a somewhat parallel case in Wagner. A form of music reached its height in him, just as another reached its zenith in Palestrina. A few attempted to carry on the Palestrina tradition, just as some men coming after Wagner tried to out-Wagner him. A German critic once caustically said in the 'nineties, apropos of this phase : " If we *must* have Richard, then let us have Wagner "—" If we *must* have Strauss, then let us have Johann ! " Debussy, too, in his book, speaks very aptly of that period when post-Wagner composers were, he says, " losing their way among sham Wotans in Hessian boots and Tristans in velvet jackets."

Following the post-Palestrina period came that wonderful stream of works of art right down to our own times. It was as quick to flow on, once it had begun, as it had been tardy in starting. Indeed, it was only in England that a hold-up occurred ; for after our great Elizabethans, and Purcell, England failed for a long time to give us any outstanding musical works.

I now propose to deal with melody. Our England has apparently always been the home of melody, for did not the King of Hungary in 1400 say to us, " Farewell with glorious victory, Blessed England full of melody." What a tribute to our folk-songs !

I wonder what constitutes original melody ? It is important not to confuse the term with air, tune or theme. Those are complete in themselves, notably folk-songs, set-songs, etc. In the early days of vocal music recitative played an important part, and sometimes developed or drifted into a sort of melody. In Bach recitative often merges into real melody of great beauty. When the earlier composers introduced secular tunes into the churches they were, in their primitive way, striving after tune-fulness, and did not know where to turn for it. There was nothing to imitate.

A not-altogether unsimilar phase is going on to-day, at a lower level. But not in the churches. The makers of popular dance music, frankly owning up to their lack of original ideas, quietly take an existing air and "jazz" it. Only the other day I heard Dvořák's beautiful "Songs my mother taught me" jazzed out of hearth and home, turned into a commonplace tune by the still more commonplace arranger. This is, of course, only a type of one of the many shams for which commercial art has always found a market, and not only in our art, but also amongst the other arts. I am no enemy of what is called ugliness when it is sincere, because then it often becomes attractive. But when an insane uproar is poured out, by a jazz band, like a foul smell, then it is offensive, as it is not made with any artistic intention.

Composers are not always thieves : they are sometimes generous donors. Apropos of this, the following is a true story. One day an English composer was playing a new work to another English composer. At a certain point he stopped playing and said to his friend, " I cannot get this stretch right—what I want here is just that type of passage you played me the other day in your new work which I liked so much." " My dear fellow," responded the other, " I am not going to finish that piece ; in fact, I have abandoned it altogether, so you are very welcome to that bit if you want it." The offer was accepted and the passage interpolated. In due course it was published, and successfully and frequently played. One day the composer went to Covent Garden and was much surprised to hear in a work of Puccini the very passage that his friend had so generously given him !

To return to recitative : in Wagner his so-called *sprechgesang* is often highly melodious. Although possessing the characteristics of recitative, it approaches the shape of a song and is in every sense of the word melodious. I could never understand how some musicians could have found Wagner devoid of melody. The prize song in *Die Meistersinger* is surely one of the greatest tunes ever written. I think our modern idea of melody grew out of the old recitative.

The other day I heard a Monteverde opera given. In it there were few actual arias, or set tunes. The dialogue was set, dramatically, to an arioso type of recitative. So long as music was self-contained as an art, which had or made no reference to things outside itself, the scale of melody, harmony and dissonances was limited. As music, little by little, became more and more the interpreter of the emotions, more dissonances grew to be used. Monteverde was evidently a pioneer in this respect also.

One feels that composers have been striving to write melodiously for the past three hundred years, and with varying success. I think the greatest composers have been those who have given us the greatest melodies. Melody is musical phraseology. Usually vulgar tunes represent vulgar harmony. The two are to be found hand in hand ; the one produces the other.

Many great composers based their melodies often upon simple harmonic progressions. Now it seems to me that this method is well-nigh, if not quite, exhausted. The return to it on the part of some young composers, especially of the French school, seems strangely stale and banal. It is, of course, not in any sense original, nor can it lead anywhere. I prefer to see, amongst our own men, a more subtle construction of melody growing up, becoming less defined, without becoming eccentric or diffuse.

Melody has gone through many ups and downs, in more senses than one, and will probably go through many more. As I said, in the past it has more often been derived from harmony, and often dependent on it. For instance, it is difficult not to believe that Beethoven had the chord of E in his mind when he thought of the first subject of the Eroica Symphony. Melody seems to be either the top of a series of chords, changing harmonies, or constructed of various notes of the same chord— or a combination of the two.

There was a certain school of composers, not very long ago, to whom an ordinary common chord was a thing so naked that it had to be shunned. When by chance one did crop up, it had to be decently robed with a wrong note or two, even at the end of a composition.

This remark was made to me the other day for the hundredth time : " In these days, when more music is being written than has ever been written before, one cannot help thinking that it must be a very difficult matter for composers to find anything new to say." It is true that our present scale of thirteen notes— and I am really making them a present of one note—has been used for some hundreds of years, and during that period many thousands of composers have rung the changes on them. Yet even to-day it sometimes happens that one is struck by a melody that has all the appearance of freshness. What, then, constitutes originality, and how is it arrived at in the circumstances? For although there are doubtless countless combinations and permutations of these thirteen notes, the number of composers who have used them through the ages must be far greater! Very likely Adam and Eve could sing them all, and no doubt there were birds as well as serpents in the Garden of Eden. We know that Orpheus must have made notes, as well as trees,[1] with his lute, and St. Francis had a taste for arranging the songs of birds. I wonder if some of our modern jazz merchants realise, and the " new " composers too, that, in spite of saxophones, savisophones, and xylophones, their tunes may be as old as ancient Rome, and that their syncopations and harmonies of to-day do not really make them " new " at all? But perhaps I do them an injustice, as they so frankly quote from the great masters occasionally. In a successful musical play, the run of which has just finished, the best tune was undoubtedly, consciously or unconsciously, by Schumann, out of the concerto.

Yet, as I said, there is originality cropping up to-day, as, indeed, there always has been. But this originality has really very little to do with the actual sequence of notes in a melodic line. For instance, Beethoven's opening to his Sonata Pathétique, the first three notes of the minor scale, is, as far as the notes are concerned, identical with the introductory phrase of Tschaikovsky's Pathetic Symphony. In spite of the mood being to a certain extent similar, these works were as " original " when they first appeared as they are to-day. No, it is the rhythmic arrangement, the harmonic and general treatment, that makes Tschaikovsky's phrase not even reminiscent of Beethoven.

The latter part of the Beethoven introduction seems very clearly to be the forerunner of the love theme in *Tristan*. In many of Wagner's heroic themes, which seem to be of extraordinary rhythmic originality, and indeed are of the greatest originality, there can be traced a superficial resemblance to many an ancient trumpet call. Their originality lies in the treatment, and the rhythmic and harmonic environment of the themes. All the greatest composers, and many of the lesser ones, have said something new in their time. From before the days

---

[1] " Orpheus with his lute made trees," the first line of the song in Shakespeare's *Henry VIII* (Act III, Scene 1), the last three lines of which are inscribed on Norman O'Neill's memorial tablet at Golders Green.—D. H.

of Purcell down to after Stravinsky new and original ideas have appeared, although I have my doubts if some of the latest modern products have even as much to do with music as the latest " Blue " or " Black Bottom," and heaven knows that is little enough !

A thing that strikes serious musicians to-day is that a great deal of what is turned out by the so-called " New School " lacks what has constituted the chief ingredient of music for all time. And that is emotion. Call it melody, harmony or rhythm, as you will. What it really is, is a combination of all three. One often hears it stated that a genius is not appreciated in his own time. Wagner is often cited as an instance of this. Although a certain school disapproved of his music, he was most assuredly appreciated by the first musicians of his own day, including representatives of such vastly different schools as Liszt, Bulow and Schumann.

Looking into the future, if I dare, I think I see signs of a more subtle construction of musical periods (perhaps the wish is father to the thought) and melody less confined, and not diffuse. I believe it to be inexhaustible. The great composers of the past, and some composers of to-day, have not been afraid of writing a simple tune because somebody with only a superficial grasp might refer to some purely unimportant and outward resemblance to some previously written work. The world is full of these hunters after reminiscence, as Weingartner aptly called them.

One feels grateful, for the *bon mot*, to the French critic who referred to Saint-Saëns as ReminisSaint-Saëns ; but he clearly gave himself away, showing how superficial was his appreciation of the art of which he was supposed to be a critic. I have come across people who, on hearing the Dominant and Tonic played in succession, say " Ha, ha—Wagner ! "

Influence, no doubt, plays a very large part in a composer's development. The greatest have been they who assimilated the work of others gone before them, adapted it to their own particular musical natures and outfit, and used it for their own purposes. Probably most composers are born with some originality. The greatest are those who have the gift of developing that particular " germ," discarding everything that is not of value to them, but retaining all that is. This is often an unconscious process. Wagner wrote : " The representative impulse of the artist's nature is altogether unconscious and instinctive. Even when in the act of moulding the product of his intuition into an objective work of art, the choice of his expression is strictly determined, not by reasoning faculty, but by the instinctive impulse which characterises his personal talent." I think one may say he is the passive instrument of a power not exactly his own. Now Wagner, who was probably the greatest of musical geniuses, assimilated the extraordinary modern ideas of Liszt, and in his later works brought them to marvellous fruition. There we have a case of a smaller man, as it were, having an enormous influence on a successor far greater than himself. Those who have heard Liszt's " Faust " Symphony cannot but have noticed this influence.

It may truly be said that the more modern composers show the influence of their immediate forebears to a greater extent than did the earlier composers. This cannot be only because to-day there is a greater opportunity of gaining a wide knowledge of contemporary music as well as that of the past. It is more probable that it has become more and more difficult to be what is called original, that is, to evolve something new after all that has been said before. I think that Richard Strauss shows the influence of Wagner more strongly than, for instance, Wagner shows the influence of Weber, or of Liszt. Here again it is easy for a " reminiscence hunter " to find such trivial likenesses as the melody in *Der Freischutz* to some of the early Wagner themes. (The trio of the *Tannhäuser* march at once occurs to one.) Now Beethoven shows only to a limited extent the influence of Mozart and Haydn, except in his early works. When the process of assimilation had taken place the originality of the musical personality showed itself in the ripe and mature work of the late Wagner and Beethoven. It seems as if, almost always, composers begin their musical life speaking the language of their predecessors, and if they are destined to be of the élite evolve their originality by this, perhaps unconscious, process of assimilation. There have been but few exceptions to this. Chopin was one.

Curiously enough, the exceptions are not to be found amongst the greatest figures. Grieg evolved a personal style of melody which was quite frankly based on Norwegian folk-song. But out of that, quite early in his career, grew an original type of harmonic treatment. In a way it grew actually out of the melodic line. It was destined to have a very considerable influence.

This really important harmonic achievement was his then-novel treatment of certain chords, notably that of the chord of the ninth and its inversions. From it grew, without doubt, the harmony of Debussy, Delius and Ravel.

The folk-song and folk-dance is again to-day playing no unimportant part in the musical development of the people.

It is influencing some composers, too, who have turned to folk-song for their inspiration, just as Grieg did. Whether any of them will evolve a style as original as Grieg's still remains to be seen. I am a little afraid it may prove a blind alley. Our English composer, Vaughan Williams, who has adopted and made our folk-song, so to speak, his own, has imitators who will find themselves in the predicament of some of those smaller followers of Grieg—in a blind alley. Grieg adopted, nay, more than that, he made folk-song his own. And a very happy marriage it was. Composing on a small canvas, making great harmonic strides, he was a composer of outstanding originality. His immediate successors, Debussy and Ravel, developed styles of their own which were of great individuality and even greater originality than Grieg's. There we have a modern instance of a smaller man having a strong influence on successors who proved to be bigger figures in the art of music than he himself had been. He stands in much the same relationship to them that Liszt did to Wagner. Musical history, like other history, has a way of repeating itself.

Actual imitators seldom lead us anywhere, for they usually only adopt the musical mannerisms of some great composer, probably because they are unable to grasp the profounder characteristics of the master. What appear to some of us to be only wild eccentricities in some of the ultra-modern school composers of to-day may well be the beginning of some great new movement, or development of our art. One must not forget that first-rate musicians condemned the work of Wagner when it appeared. One heard the same epithets hurled at him as one hears to-day : " No melody, no harmony, sheer ugliness ! "

Those contemporaries of Wagner were no doubt quite sincere, and I must say I feel much less in sympathy with them than I do with the severe critics of some of the very latest native, and imported, noises. But, as I said before, these very noises, as we hear them, may be the forerunners of some quite serious and notable development. Time will prove what importance, or otherwise, they have.

Do we find strong characteristics in our contemporary composers to-day ? Yes and no—this is dangerous ground— more " no " than " yes," perhaps. Is the music of Debussy and Ravel as widely contrasted as that of Brahms and Dvořák ? Or, if I dare say so, that of Holst and Vaughan Williams and Bax ? I could talk for much longer than you would care to hear me on these points, and must leave them for some other

time lest I stray away too far from my theme, a formal mistake
which no composer should make.

In all well-appointed compositions, after development some
thought or hinting at a recapitulation occurs. This, as the
tight-rope walker said, we call " Balance." And you will no
doubt begin to feel that happy sense of relief one has when he
reaches the ground safely, that sense which anticipates a speedy
conclusion. But I warn you not to be too optimistic. Some,
and classical composers, have a way of piling coda on coda—
a rather exasperating device. I asked Humperdinck once when
a coda began in a famous work. " I really can't say," he said,
" the last half seems all codas ! "

Yes—it is vastly more difficult to be what is called original
to-day. It may be we have no great giants—no Bachs, Beethovens,
or Wagners—amongst us. I do not know. The test is, no doubt,
the greatest test of all : the test of time.

Many people hold the opinion that music should be heard
but not talked, or written, about. I certainly think we read
rather too much about music to-day ; but I do think that it is
of great interest when composers like Wagner, Berlioz, and
Debussy put their opinions on paper. The latter was a great
critic, although he has been hauled over the coals for his book,
Mr. Croche the Dilettante Hater. I think musical critics rather
resent musicians poaching on their preserves ! I trust they will
not think I am doing so !

The power of criticism is in nobody so strong as in a genuine
creative artist. This power, with discernment, balance, and
above all the gift of God he was born with, builds the originality
we find in the great men of our art. We must not forget that
originality of melody does not altogether depend on the actual
sequence of notes. A given series, put together in the year 1927,
may be identical with one of 1827, and yet have all the qualities
of freshness. It is an old commonplace to say that the giant
composers were the only originators. Many lesser lights have
been that, as, for instance, Grieg, that link between the older
and the newer schools. It is together that all " Men of Notes "
make up that stream of melody that has flowed ever since the
world began. If the advanced school of to-day—I hesitate to
call any of them giants—is not doing much to keep that fountain
flowing, then, at least, the lesser lights, even our jazzing friends,
are endeavouring to pour out some sort of tune. And lesser
lights have been of the greatest service to the development of
composition.

One of the greatest, perhaps the greatest, living composer,

once said to me : "After all, music is a very delicate affair."
One wishes that musicians, critics and the public would remember that and treat it with more gentleness than they sometimes
do.   Nothing seems to me more absurd than to run down the
great master works of the present or past.   I do not mean to say
that anybody is not perfectly entitled to say : " Beethoven,
Wagner or Stravinsky do not appeal to *me*."   He may be tired
of them, or not in touch with them.   But for all that, a great
work of art remains a great work of art, however hackneyed it
may become, and in spite of fads and fashions should be " a joy
for ever."   I trust our country always may be " Blessed England,
full of melody."

LIST OF COMPOSITIONS

I am grateful to many of these publishers for their help in preparing this list.

D. H.

ORCHESTRAL WORKS

Date	Opus	Title	Publisher
1893–7	3	Suite for Strings.	
1901	8	Overture : " In Autumn."	
1903–4	11	Overture : *Hamlet*.	
1904		Dirge from *Hamlet*.	
1904	14	Miniatures for small orchestra.	
1905–6	21	Overture : " In Springtime."	
1908	25	Miniatures. Six pieces for full orchestra.	
1910	29	Theme and Variations on an Irish Air (Orchestral version of op. 17 for two pianos).	
1911	30	A Scotch Rhapsody, for full orchestra.	
1913	43	Introduction, Mazurka and Finale. (From " A Forest Idyll.")	
1913	47	Overture : " Humoresque."	
1916	48	Hornpipe . . . . Published for piano and for full and small orchestra.	Bos
1923		" Irish Jig." For chamber orchestra.	
1924		" Punch and Judy." . . . . . Published for full and small orchestra. Also for piano.	AHC
1925		Three Exotic Dances for full orchestra. (From *Kismet*.)	
1925		Fairy-Tale Suite. (From *Through the Green Door*.)	

ORCHESTRAL WORKS (continued)

Date	Opus	Title	Publisher
1926		" Alice in Wonderland."	
1927		" Festal Prelude."	Bos
		Published for piano and for full and small orchestra.	
1928		Two Shakespearean Sketches	C
		Published for full and small orchestra : (i) Nocturne ; (ii) Masquerade.	
		Pastorale for strings.	

CHORUS AND ORCHESTRA

1905	19	" Waldemar."	
		Fantasy for solo voices, chorus, and orchestra.	
1909	34	Eight national songs arranged for unison chorus and orchestra.	

SOLO VOICE AND ORCHESTRA

1904	12	" Death on the Hills."	
		Ballad for contralto and orchestra.	
1908	31	" La Belle Dame sans Merci."	
		For baritone and full orchestra.	
1930		" The Farmer and the Fairies."	
		Words by Herbert Asquith. A recitation with orchestral or piano accompaniment.	

OTHER CHORAL WORKS

1914		" Noel " : A Carol	S & B
		Words by Hilaire Belloc. For S.A.T.B. and bells ad lib.	
1918		" Lullaby." Two-part song . . .	Arn
1922		" Come Away Death." Part song. . .	G
		(From The Merchant of Venice.)	
1925		" The Moon is Up." Unison song . .	C
		Words by Alfred Noyes.	
1927		" The West Countree." Unison song .	C
		Words by Sir Harold Boulton.	
1928		" Come, Tuneful Friends." . . .	C
		Four-part song in the Victorian manner. Words by Sir Harold Boulton.	
1928		" Mount and Away ! " Two-part song .	JW
		Words by Sir Harold Boulton.	

OTHER CHORAL WORKS (*continued*)

Date	Opus	Title	Publisher
1933		" The Music of the Waves "	JW

For mixed-voice choir. S.A.T.B. Words by
Sir Harold Boulton.
" Dirge for the Year."
By Shelley. Part song for women's voices and
stringed orchestra.
" Moon Roses."
A Scottish song-scena for two voices, harp and
string quartet.

SOLO SONGS

Date	Opus	Title	Publisher
1896		" Parted "	W
1898		" A Norse Lullaby "	B
		Words by Eugene Field.	
1899		" The Light of Love "	B
		Words by Hartley Coleridge.	
1899		Two songs : " Roses in the Garden," " A Prayer "	F
1900		" The Indian Serenade "	R
		Words by Shelley.	
1902		" Madelaine's Song "	B
		(From *After All*.)	
1904	16	Two songs : " When You Come," " A Modern Greek Song." (Also orchestrated.)	S
1907	18	Five Rondels for medium voice : " Rondeau " (W. E. Henley) ; " The Lilacs are in Bloom " (George Moore) ; " The Lovely Isle," " A Roundel of Rest " (Arthur Symons) ; " With Strawberries " (W. E. Henley).	A
1907	26	Two French songs : " Un Grand Sommeil Noire " (Verlaine), " Ballade Française	A
1909			
1909	35 (i)	" Love in the Cherry Tree "	S
1909	35 (ii)	" Where be you going, you Devon Maid ? " . (Keats.)	S
1911		" All for me "	B
1913		" Håkon's Lullaby " . . . . . (From *The Pretenders*.)	E
1918		" Eagles of England "	E
		Words by P. Bewsher. Dedicated to the R.A.F.	
1919		" The Warrior Love "	S
		Words by Sir William Watson.	
1920		Six songs from *Through the Green Door* : .	A-F
1920		(i) " Through the Green Door " ; (ii) " The Cat's Song " ; (iii) " Molly's Song " ; (iv) " Silvery Dreams " ; (v) " Rikk's Song " ; (vi) " The Princess's Song."	

SOLO SONGS (continued)

Date	Opus	Title	Publisher
1920		"The Song of Lucius" . . . . . (From *Julius Cæsar* ; words from "Lucrece.")	A-F
1921		"Yo, ho, ho, and a Bottle of Rum" . . . (Sung in *Ambrose Applejohn's Adventure*.)	KP
1922		"Tell me where is Fancy Bred" . . . (From *The Merchant of Venice*.)	G
1922		"It was a Lover and his Lass" . . . (From *The Merchant of Venice*.)	G
1923		"Musette" . . . . (From *A Roof and Four Walls*.)	C
1923		"On a Grey Day" . . . . . Words by E. Temple Thurston. (From *A Roof and Four Walls*.)	C
1924		Blossom Songs . . . . . . (From the Japanese.) Accompaniment for piano and string quartet.	C
1924		"A Song Cycle" . . . . . Words by E. Temple Thurston. (i) Cuckoo ; (ii) Wren ; (iii) Wagtail ; (iv) Night-jar ; (v) Woodpecker.	C
1925		"The Golden Hour of Noon" . . . Words by Ashley Dukes. (From *The Man with a Load of Mischief*.)	C
1925		"I have a Flaunting Air" . . . . Words by Ashley Dukes. (From *The Man with a Load of Mischief*.)	C
1925		Three songs from *Kismet* : . . . "Lo ! still the stars" ; "Lute Song" ; "Marsinah's Song."	KP
1926		"Echoes of Erin" . . . . . Twelve Irish songs. Words by Sir Harold Boulton. Irish translation by Dr. Douglas Hyde. (i) "The Piping on the Hill" ; (ii) "Biddy, I'm not Jesting" ; (iii) "When Fergus smote the Shield" ; (iv) "Lullaby, Lilybud" ; (v) "Conn and the Merrow Maid" ; (vi) "What Anybody Knows" ; (vii) "The Pretty Girl Milking Her Cow" ; (viii) "The Yellow Boreen" ; (ix) "Eileen" ; (x) "I Know an Isle" ; (xi) "Barney the Piper" ; (xii) "Exile's Song."	B
1930		"Jewels"	Ro
1931		"May Lilies"	C
1931		"When May walks by"	C
1934		"Home of Mine"	C

CHAMBER MUSIC

Date	Opus	Title	Publisher
1895	1	Variations on " Pretty Polly Oliver " for piano, violin and 'cello.	
1896	2	'Cello and piano sonata.	
1897	6	Scherzo and Romance for piano and violin.	
1900	7	Trio in A Minor for piano, violin and 'cello.	
1902–3	10	Quintet for strings and piano.	
1909	32	Trio in F for piano, violin and 'cello, in one movement	S
1909	33	Berceuse for violin and piano accompaniment .	S
	52	Scherzo for string quartet.	
1921		Two pieces for violin and piano . . .	S
		(i) " Celtic Legend " ; (ii) " Nocturne."	
1922		" Running Water."	
		For quintet, also for piano (see Piano Music.)	
		" Biddy, I'm not Jesting." For quintet.	
		" Valse Gracieuse." For quintet.	

PIANO MUSIC

Date	Opus	Title	Publisher
1898	4	Four compositions for piano	F
		Allegro grazioso ; Allegro agitato ; Adagio espressivo ; Allegro scherzando.	
1898	5	Variations and Fugue for piano.	
1904	15	Three piano pieces	S
		Caprice ; Intermezzo ; Burlesque.	
1905	17	Variations and Fugue on an Irish theme for two pianos	S
		(Orchestrated as op. 29.)	
1906	20	Three pieces for piano	S
		Berceuse ; Valse ; Gavotte.	
1911	24 (i)	" A Memory "	
1911	24 (ii)	Toccata study for piano	E
1919		Three Old English pieces for piano . . .	S
		" Real Morris " ; " Rigadoon " ; " Elizabethan March."	
1919	50 (ii)	" Carillon "	AHC
		(Also published in Braille.)	
1922		Two Entr'actes for piano	S
		" Running Water " (Also for quintet) ; " Ragtime." (A Cockney tune.)	
1924		" A Landscape "	Arn
1927		Suite for piano	KP
		Theme ; Romance ; Intermezzo ; Ragtime.	
1928		Three sketches for piano	Ro

PIANO MUSIC FOR CHILDREN

Date	Opus	Title	Publisher
1908	27	Two easy pieces for piano	S
		Romance ; Gigue.	
1918		Four songs without words	A-F
1919		" In the Branches ".	A-F
		Four easy pieces.	
1921		Four easy pieces	A-F
1923		Four little Dances	A-F
		Gopak ; Habanera ; Valse ; Ragtime.	
1926		Four tunes for the sea	I
1928		Four syncopated pieces	JW
		(Arab Dance published separately, 1928.)	
1929		Four country pictures	OUP
1930		" All Fours." Duets	OUP
1930		" The King's House." Suite . . .	LGB
1933		Three piano duets	OUP

INCIDENTAL MUSIC TO THE FOLLOWING PLAYS (among others)

1901–2		After All.	B
		" Madelaine's Song " published.	
1902		The Exile.	
1904	13	Hamlet.	
1906	22	A Lonely Queen.	
1907	23	The Spell (A Tragedy of Truth).	
1908	28	The Bride of Lammermoor (The Last Heir).	
1909		The World and his Wife.	
1909	36	King Lear.	
1909	37	The Blue Bird	E
		" Song of the Mothers " published ; " Dance of the Joys," Four Dances, "The Blue Bird Waltz," and a selection published for piano ; Four Dances and " The Blue Bird Waltz " published for orchestra. Dances arr. for piano and strings by A. Reynolds (pubd. 1941).	
1910		Priscilla Runs Away	Ch
		Waltz, " Priscilla," published for piano.	
1911	39	All that Matters.	
1911	41	The Gods of the Mountain	S
		Two dances : Dance of Wine and Sacrificial Dance, published for piano.	
1912	44	The Golden Doom.	
1913	45	The Pretenders	E
		Håkon's Lullaby published.	
1914		The Holy City.	
1916	51	Paddly Pools.	
1918		Freedom.	
1918–19		Through the Green Door	A-F
		Six songs published (see Solo Songs).	

INCIDENTAL MUSIC TO THE FOLLOWING PLAYS (continued)

Date	Opus	Title	Publisher
1919		Reparation	AHC
		" Reparation " Waltz, published for piano ; Russian Gipsy Songs published.	
1920		Julius Cæsar	A-F
		Song of Lucius published.	
1920		Mary Rose	S
		Preludes and interludes and the Call published for piano, and Prelude and Call for orchestra.	
1920		Macbeth.	
1921		The Knave of Diamonds	KP
		Suite published for piano.	
1921		The Love Thief.	
1921		Quality Street	S
		Eight arrangements of dances published for piano.	
1922		The Way of an Eagle.	
1922		The Merchant of Venice	G
		Three songs published. (See under Solo Songs and under Other Choral Works.)	
1922		Stigmata.	
1923		Via Crucis.	
1923		Success.	
1923		The Prisoner of Zenda	C
		Incidental music published for piano, and Intermezzo " Flavia " for small orchestra.	
1924		A Kiss for Cinderella	C
		Incidental music published for piano.	
1925		Kismet	KP
		Three songs published (see under Solo Songs) and three dances published for piano : Egyptian Dance, Marsinah's Dance, Indian Dance.	
1925		The Man with a Load of Mischief . . .	C
		Two songs published (see under Solo Songs).	
1925		Cristilinda.	
1927		The White Chateau.	
1928		Mr. Pickwick.	
1929		The Lady with the Lamp.	
1929		The Ivory Door.	
1929		The Shadow of the East.	
1929		Measure for Measure.	
1930		To Meet the King !	
1931		Little Catherine.	
1932		Man Overboard.	
1933		Francis Thompson.	
1933		This Side Idolatry.	
1933		Acropolis.	
1933		Henry V.	

BALLETS

Date	Opus	Title	Publisher
1913	43	" A Forest Idyll."	
1917		" Before Dawn "	B
		Interlude published for piano and for full and small orchestra.	
1921		" The Snow Queen."	
1924		" Punch and Judy "	AHC
		(From *The Punch Bowl*.) Published for piano and for full and small orchestra.	
1926		" Alice in Lumberland "	FDH
		From *R.S.V.P.* Published for piano.	

ARRANGEMENTS

1906–31		Ten eighteenth-century pieces by J. H. Fiocco .	S
		Nos. 1–7 arranged by Norman O'Neill and Arthur Bent : (i) Arioso, (ii) La Legere, (iii) Allegro, (iv) Allemande, (v) L'Anglaise, (vi) Menuetto, (vii) La Fringante ; remainder arr. by Norman O'Neill : (viii) Rondo, (ix) Deux Gavottes, (x) L'Inconstante.	
1920		Three-Fours, by S. Coleridge Taylor . . .	Au
		Valse suite. Orchestrated by Norman O'Neill.	

BOOKS

1903		*A Golden Treasury of Song.* (Vol. I) . . .	B
		Edited by Norman O'Neill.	
1905		*Ethical Hymn Book with Music*	O
		Issued by the Council of the Union of Ethical Societies. Musical Editor, Norman O'Neill.	
1906		*A Song-Garden for Children*	Arn
		Music edited and arranged by Norman O'Neill.	
1916		Dramatised scenes from Longfellow's " Hiawatha "	Keg
		By Valerie Wingate, with music by Norman O'Neill.	
1926		*Echoes of Erin*	B
		The music arranged by Norman O'Neill. (*See under* Solo Songs.)	

INDEX